The
CARLING
YEARS

The
CARLING
YEARS

England Rugby 1988–96

Mick Cleary

photographs by Colorsport

VICTOR GOLLANCZ
LONDON

First published in Great Britain 1996
by Victor Gollancz
An imprint of the Cassell Group
Wellington House, 125 Strand, London, WC2R ORB

A catalogue record for this book is
available from the British Library.

ISBN 0 575 06402 1

Produced by Lennard Books
A division of Lennard Associates Limited
Mackerye End, Harpenden, Herts, AL5 5DR

Editor (for Lennard Books): Marion Paull
Production Editor: Chris Hawkes
Design Consultants: Design 2 Print
Reproduction: CMYK Graphics Ltd

Printed and bound in Slovenia

Contents

Acknowledgement

The author acknowledges the following sources
for quotes reported in this book:

Will Carling: The Authorised Biography – Ian Norrie (Headline, 1993)
Brian Moore: The Autobiography – Brian Moore, with Stephen Jones (Partridge Press, 1995)
High Balls and Happy Hours – Gavin Hastings, with Clem Thomas (Mainstream, 1994)

Introduction

You could always tell an English rugby player. There he stood, tall, erect, square-chinned and hopelessly self-conscious. He had so many advantages, so much to recommend him, and yet when it came to the crunch he would wilt. England's record of under-achievement from the beginning of the sixties through to the late eighties was quite staggering. They had more players at their disposal than any other nation. They had more schools, larger clubs and greater resources than anyone else, all of which counted for nothing. On 19 January 1963, England travelled to Cardiff and won 13–6, Malcolm Phillips and John Owen scoring tries, the peerless Richard Sharp weighing in with two conversions and a dropped goal. There were seven new caps in the side. Other than that the only significant historical note of the match was that the conditions were mercilessly cold and unforgiving. The ink froze in many of the pens scribbling this routine tale in the press box. That same year England went on to take the championship.

It was to be another twenty-eight years before the journalists were to record the next English victory in Cardiff. In that same period they were to win the championship only once outright, Billy Beaumont's famous gathering of diehards delivering the goods in 1980. It was a long barren stretch, a time of too much rueful scratching of heads and shrugging of shoulders and not enough decisive action. The broad consensus seemed to be that it was a mere cycle of history, a spin of nature's capricious wheel which would one day come round again and all would be well. The wheel spun and spun and it never did come right.

No matter how often the Englishmen called upon their innate phlegm in times of crisis, how often they thrust out the stiff upper lip and pretended it didn't matter, you knew that deep down they were utterly baffled. Why should this have been so? There were many theories.

'Too many sweatbands, not enough sweat,' was the grizzled, and not entirely inaccurate, assessment of New Zealand's old warhorse, Colin Meads. Pinetree, as he was known, had every right to be dismissive, for he was the epitome of the All Black brotherhood, one which never yielded an inch on a rugby field and which willingly gave over body and soul to the cause. It wasn't that Englishmen weren't prepared to take their own share of bumps and bruises for the old country. In nearly every way they were as brave, as strong and as resilient as their opponents; in every way bar one – the inner man was nowhere near as hard.

Time and again England, particularly in Cardiff, had the form book in their favour. Time and again they flunked the test, overcome by a lack of deep belief in themselves. Perhaps also there was a fear, an embarrassment, of taking it too seriously; or rather being seen to take it too seriously. After all, it was only a game. But you knew that it hurt. You could tell by the slumped shoulders and deadened eyes. England were not afraid of the opposition; they were afraid of themselves. They knew that they should win but they didn't know how. The opportunity was there on so many occasions. Instead of grasping it, they allowed the moment to taunt and mock them. The Welsh made an art form of it. England could talk a good game; they were unable to play one.

The only times they came close to redressing the balance was when the pressure was off, when they were not expected to win. Then they would play with relish and even abandon, defying the odds stacked against them. Slip a tag of favourites round their neck and they would shrivel at the prospect. This was never the way of any of the other major rugby-playing countries. The South Africans have long been openly rebuked for their apparent arrogance. The history of their blighted country is based on the notion of supremacy of the white man. Rugby is the white man's game, the embodiment of his

The man charged with changing the face of English rugby – Geoff Cooke.

Black has a duty to uphold the tradition.

'They play to repay the debt they owe those who have striven and suffered to create the history and fuel the mystery,' said David Kirk, their World Cup-winning captain of 1987, as articulate off the field as he was influential on it. For a New Zealander, losing was never an option, for it shamed not just fifteen men but an entire nation.

Australians have a different motivation but a similar purpose. Their culture is brash, aggressive and unpretentious. Sport is an expression of their boisterous tendencies. Put an Englishman in a sporting arena and in a favourable position and he seemed almost to apologise for being there, for having the temerity to take it so seriously as perhaps to win. Cricket, soccer or rugby, it has always been the same. The Celtic countries have never had to suffer this torment, for their story has always been that of the underdog, of the little man who tired of being trampled underfoot and scrapped his way to the top of the pile.

So much for the inner traumas. There were also practical reasons why England were so hopelessly unproductive during this time. The most cursory of glances at their teamsheets will tell you all you need to know about the inadequacies of their selection policy. In fact a cursory glance is impossible. Sheet after sheet of names, a roll-call of competent sportsmen betrayed by a woeful system, indicates no continuity, no direction and no planning. If it didn't work the first time the only course of action was to change it. There was no sense of developing the long-term, only a frantic snatch at the short-term. The revolving-door policy created generation after generation of anxious players. They knew better than anyone that if they didn't get it right they would be out in the wilderness straight afterwards. And the selectors wondered why their men played as if the world was pressing down on their shoulders.

Take a look at some of the names who pulled on the white shirt in hope during those indecisive times, only to retreat in despair some matches later. Take a look in particular at those poor put-upon souls called upon to save the mother country at half back. There were eight

ruggedness and simple, singular beliefs. Times and attitudes have mercifully changed, or at least they have in the political arena and in many areas in the country at large. On a rugby field it's business as usual.

The New Zealanders are fuelled by a deep-rooted desire to prove that they are a nation of significance. Rugby has often been the means to that end. The country from the end of the earth wants to be noticed. The All Blacks have been the standard-bearers of their people. If they were to flinch when the pressure came on, their country would flinch too. Kiwis are a stern, hard, serious race. They play their rugby in the same way. Every All

scrum halves used in the seventies alone: Nigel Starmer-Smith started off the decade, to be followed by Jacko Page, Jan Webster, Lionel Weston, Steve Smith, Peter Kingston, Malcolm Young and Mike Lampkowski. In the eighties it was the turn of the fly halves to be put into the blender: John Horton, Huw Davies, Les Cusworth, Stuart Barnes, Peter Williams and, finally, Rob Andrew. What is worse is that there was so little sense of collective and considered strategy. Les Cusworth was famed throughout the land as a running fly half. He was duly selected and instructed to kick.

No wonder that England lost their way. Out they would come year after year, convinced that this was the season when they would get it right. Like some mad professor locked away in his chaotic laboratory, the England selectors ploughed on head down, fired by the misguided belief that sooner or later they would chance upon the magic formula. Only once did it all come together. Finally, after suffering so much together, those great old servants of the game, Billy Beaumont, Roger Uttley, Fran Cotton, Tony Neary and Steve Smith, put the show together themselves and won England the Grand Slam. The following year it was back to familiar territory; won two, lost two.

The whole desperate situation eventually came to a head at the first World Cup in 1987. It was a marvellous tournament, one which kicked off with Australia beating England 19–6 in Sydney, England's captain that day, Mike Harrison, doing his bit in scoring his side's only try. Even in defeat England offered signs of hope. They went on to beat Japan, 60–7, and the USA, 34–6, in their other group matches to qualify for a quarter-final match against Wales. This time there was no Cardiff bogey to allay, no psychological demons to haunt them. What is more, Wales were dogged by injury, so much so that they had to resort to the tactic favoured by many pub touring teams of the past and summon one of the boys from the beach. David Young, the 19-year-old prop, was not called up on merit but simply because he was on holiday in Canberra. In went the young prop and backwards went the first English scrum. It wasn't by much against a tape measure but in that key arena, the mind, the little nudge stretched

across a canyon. Wales went on to win 16–3, with tries by Roberts, Jones and Devereux. England had once again been crippled by great expectations.

That day was a low point in English rugby history. It may also have been the key turning point. England trudged home. The management team of Mike Weston and Martin Green departed and Geoff Cooke arrived at the helm. There has been so much success for England in the nineties that it would be easy to think that it all slotted into place as soon as Cooke tucked his feet under the manager's chair. So efficient, so thorough, so slick and so professional did England's approach become, that it's difficult to remember when it wasn't so. But the long catalogue of failure outlined here did happen and might well have carried on happening if it had not been for Cooke's intervention. His was an unheralded appointment in October 1987. To many he was just another name, another selector, another manager who would offer the same qualities as many of his predecessors: endeavour, steadfastness, integrity and worthiness. But success? That was quite another question. Cooke appeared to be no different from any who had gone before. Born on 11 June 1941, he had scaled no great heights, playing as a stand off or centre for Bradford and Cumberland. He captained both club and county, later moving on to become secretary and coach to Bradford. He was Yorkshire coach for five years and a divisional selector from 1979–86. He was team manager to the North for just one year, 1986–87, before the call came to the England cause.

It was an inspired choice by the RFU, the one selection they finally got right. Cooke had double vision: the short-term was crucial in that victory built confidence, but he knew that England would achieve nothing of substance and lasting significance if deeper roots were not put down. He had his ideas but he had no blueprint. In fact it didn't come right immediately. England played well enough in the 1988 championship. They travelled to Paris for the first match, a formidable test on paper. France were the Five Nations champions and the Parc des Princes an intimidating venue. England, for whom a certain Will Carling made his début, were desperately

unlucky not to come away with a victory, losing 10–9. They lost 11–3 at Twickenham to Wales, but won 9–6 in Scotland before finishing off in style, 35–3 at home to Ireland. It augured well. Then came the disastrous tour to Australia.

Both Tests were lost, 22–16 and 28–8, but it was the wretched state of morale which most concerned Cooke. The tour was led by Bedford lock John Orwin. England had begun the season with Mike Harrison in charge. He was dropped and Nigel Melville took over the reins. He was injured and so enter Orwin. It was hoped that Orwin might develop into a Beaumont type of leader. He proved to be anything but. There was dissension in the ranks, a split between forwards and backs, dissatisfaction with the backing from the RFU.

It was time for Cooke to act. It was time for more thorough application; for radical surgery. It was time for Will Carling.

Chapter One

1988–89:
The start of a new era

Geoff Cooke knew what he wanted. Will Carling had no idea. We tend to elevate our sporting heroes on to a little celestial platform where they sit blithely immune from the woes and stresses which affect we normal, humdrum folk. Sportsmen are confident, secure, self-contained and utterly certain about their own role in life. They have no frailties and no anxieties. This is all complete garbage, of course. If anything, the opposite is usually the case. Sportsmen are one of the most neurotic, unstable bunch of people you can meet. The bit we see, the performance itself, is often an act. Long may it be like that, for sport is meant to be a theatrical interlude, a romantic distraction from the aggravation of the real world.

So it was that when Will Carling came to the phone to take a call from Geoff Cooke one Thursday evening in October 1988 his heart fluttered, not from the prospect of the wonderful news about to float down the line but at the thought that after just seven caps maybe this was the end of his career. Insecurity is an ever-present companion in a sportsman's life. Cooke, of course, was the bearer of extremely good tidings, but it took time for Carling to register the fact.

'When he told me I was actually in the side to face Australia, I was so relieved that I didn't really take in what he was saying about the captaincy,' said Carling. 'It wasn't until after I put the phone down that it hit me. I wandered around the house like a zombie.'

Carling revealed later in his biography that he was determined one day to ply himself with a suitable amount of alcohol and then sit down with Geoff Cooke to try and get a straight answer to the most puzzling question of all: 'Why the hell did you pick me?'

Cooke's choice was indeed a bolt from the blue. Carling was still in short trousers in international terms and, even though he had made a decent start to his England career, he rightly felt he had not yet decisively

made the place his own. At 22 he was the youngest man in the squad. He became the youngest England captain for fifty-seven years. There was more. Not only had he been given the honour of leading the side against Australia, he also received a vote of confidence from Cooke for the entire winter campaign and maybe many more to come.

'I have made it clear to Carling that we expect him to captain the side throughout the season,' said Cooke. 'We have had a succession of short-term captaincies. The feeling was that we had to establish an England captain who, though it is early for him, would take us through the next three seasons to the World Cup.'

No wonder Carling felt stunned. His world was about to change. Even the most agile of imaginations, however, could not have foreseen what twists and turns there would be to the tale over the next eight years. The showbusiness profile, the gossip column spotlight, old farts and princesses were all a long way off for the moment. Carling's immediate priority was quite simple: how on earth to keep the news quiet for the next two days. The squad themselves were not to be told until Saturday evening when they gathered at the Petersham Hotel in Richmond to prepare for the match against Australia the following Saturday. At the thought of meeting some of the senior pros, a small bead of sweat broke out on Carling's forehead. How the hell would a young pup still wet behind the ears face the likes of Wade Dooley and Paul Rendall, coal-face workers not given to listening to upstarts? That Carling won these men over within such a short space of time was not the least of his considerable achievements.

Even though it may not have seemed like it at the time, it was really Cooke who was under the most pressure for making Carling captain. It was the first decisive moment in Cooke's own career. Already, barely twelve months into the job, he was facing a credibility crisis. Carling

was the fifth player in that time to take on the mantle of captain. Two of those choices had been forced on Cooke by injury. Even so, in sport there are always voices in the wings wondering if the man in the middle has got it right. It's a notoriously fickle business and although rugby is nothing like as brutal as soccer in reaching for the trigger every time a manager has a sticky time, Cooke himself knew that he had to get it right on this occasion. Mike Harrison, Nigel Melville, John Orwin and Richard Harding had all had their moment over the past year. Melville, the Wasps scrum half, was, in fact, Cooke's original preference, but he was badly injured in the last match of the 1988 championship against Ireland, and never played at the same level again.

'Nigel had been my long-term choice,' said Cooke. 'He was an automatic selection at scrum half and had a good attitude.'

Cooke was determined to signal his intentions to the squad, to the RFU and to the country at large by pledging himself to someone for a long period. Cooke realized that the great bane of English rugby over the last twenty years had been instability. Hesitant selection had created nervous teams. Since Bill Beaumont's career had come to an end in 1982, through a head injury, after he had led his country a record twenty-one times, England had worked their way through nine captains. Steve Smith followed Beaumont but lasted only a year. Then came John Scott, Peter Wheeler, Melville (briefly), Paul Dodge, Richard Hill and then, in quick succession, the four chosen for various reasons by Cooke. It was time to put down some roots. But who was it to be?

In the end it boiled down to a choice between Carling and Rob Andrew. If anything Andrew had the better credentials. He had twenty caps. In many ways he was temperamentally suited to the job. He was thoughtful, intelligent, likeable, respected and, for all his head prefect appearance, every bit as fierce a competitor as someone like Brian Moore. He was also, like Cooke, a northerner. No one could fault his attitude. England coach, Roger Uttley, also found it easier to relate to Andrew. But, and it was a significant caveat, Andrew was not on top of his game and so was not guaranteed his

place. Cooke knew that the morale of his side would not stand much buffeting if the captain was under pressure for his place. The field narrowed to one. Cooke took the plunge.

It had been a bewildering few months for Carling. His arrival on the Australian tour of that summer had been delayed so that he could sit his finals at Durham University, where he was studying psychology. As a result he missed the first Test. Carling had been on an Army scholarship at Durham. His father, Bill, and brother, Marcus, were both soldiers. Will followed in his father's footsteps, serving in the Royal Regiment of Wales. By the summer of 1988, though, it was obvious that things were going to change. He had lost interest in his studies and, not surprisingly, finished with only a Recommended pass. It was becoming clear, too, that the Army were none too keen on Carling slogging up and down rugby fields when he ought to have been tramping through the mud on his initial officers' training course at Sandhurst. Something had to give, and it was the Army.

Carling bought himself out for £8,000, paid over five years. Even so it was a lot of money for a student, but Carling was determined to see it through for the simple reason that it was what he wanted to do. Not for the first time, nor the last, he made his decision and stuck with it. He came to London, joined the Harlequins full-time and took up a job as a retail marketer with Mobil Oil.

Some things about Will Carling were constant. They were true then and they are true today. He is close to his family and relies on a tight circle of friends from his schooldays at Sedbergh School in the Lake District. Carling is essentially a shy, retiring person at heart yet, somewhat paradoxically, has yearnings to lead and be in the public eye. He was an art scholar at school and still likes to sketch in his spare time. All these tendencies were there from an early age and stayed with him. One of Carling's school reports notes that his headmaster was seeing in him 'less bullishness and more consideration and leadership'. Carling had also always been a rugby player of some distinction. He played for the first XV for three years yet was only captain in the final term. In fact, he captained England Schools, in 1984, before he captained the school side. As a player, Carling's assets

stand out. He is a hard, straight, reliable and unremitting runner. At Durham University he came into contact with Ted Wood, a long-standing and much respected coach who was to be manager of the northern divisional side.

'When Will had a lot of space, he didn't look class,' said Wood. 'When the space was closed down, he began to look world-class. He presented the ball beautifully, he never missed a tackle, he's fast and he's strong.'

So much for the background. It was no different in essence from that of a hundred other young England hopefuls. While he was a mere club player, neither his character, his friends, his social life nor his qualifications were of the remotest interest to anyone else. Even in his early days with England he attracted little lasting attention. But all of a sudden it was a whole new ball game. The whole world wanted to know the full story of the young Englishman about to lead his country for the first time.

Carling had some small assistance in dodging the media spotlight. There were three new caps in the side to face Australia: Harlequins team-mates Andrew Harriman (wing) and Paul Ackford (lock) were called to the colours, as was scrum half Dewi Morris, who at that time was with Liverpool St Helens. The side had Geoff Cooke's stamp all over it. He had taken careful note of the divisional performances against the tourists and rewarded the on-form players accordingly. Cooke had spent most of his working life in sport and local government. He knew that management and planning were crucial.

'Selection had been England's biggest problem,' said Cooke. 'We had to get that right. I then wanted to involve all fifteen players so that each of them felt they had an important role to play on the field. Above all I wanted to create a situation where people enjoyed playing for England.'

Cooke was happy to stand by his side come what may. If he were to fail, then he wanted to fail on his own terms. He had already made two key selections in asking former British Lion Roger Uttley to be coach and ex-Nottingham hooker John Elliott to be a selector. Uttley and Cooke were on the same wavelength.

'New Zealanders can't believe we have so many talented players around,' said Uttley. 'When you look at some of the players who have become All Blacks, some of them are quite ordinary players. But they are all quite clear in their own minds what they have to do to achieve their end. We are not so single-minded, not so clued up about what to do in any given situation on the field. New Zealanders are all on the same wavelength.'

Cooke's long-term vision was of representative English sides who would all play in a discernible way. Of course there would be variations but there had also to be uniformity.

'It's a very long-term process,' said Cooke. 'What we are trying to do is to put in place an effective English way of playing the game, of getting a concept from the national side down.'

But first came the Australians. Despite their success against England in the 1988 summer series, the Australians had struggled on their autumn tour so far. In part this had been due to the surprising adventure, commitment and thoroughness of the divisional sides they faced. Dick Best's London side set the pattern with an invigorating and enterprising 21–10 victory in the opening match at Twickenham. Best pledged himself to an open, fluid style and his players carried it off perfectly, Mark Bailey, David Pegler and Andrew Harriman all scoring tries. The pacy, elusive Harriman, a maverick spirit, won his one and only cap as a result. Paul Ackford's call-up at the age of 30, having won his first B cap nine years earlier, was a tribute to his own perseverance, Best's shrewd club coaching and Cooke's own perceptive instincts. Within a couple of seasons, Ackford was to have no equal in the whole world as a front-jumper and athletic second-row forward. Similarly the inclusion of Dewi Morris said much about Cooke's insights into the game. Morris had barely twenty first-class games to his name yet Cooke had spotted that his tough, aggressive play would serve England's cause well.

Australia had a great track record in the British Isles. They had won the Grand Slam on their 1984 tour. This was the sixteenth match in the series against England, of which they had won ten. Australia had been comfortable double victors over England just a few months earlier yet

Will Carling offloads the ball during his first match as England captain.

this time around, without the recently retired Poidevin (who later changed his mind), Slack and Rodriguez, or Papworth and Burke, who had switched to rugby league, they were struggling. As well as the defeat by London, they lost to the North, 15–9, and the South-West, 26–10. Their only real showing of form came at Sale with the comprehensive win over England B, 37–10. Any side fielding Farr-Jones, Lynagh, who had only just joined the tour, and the mercurial Campese, was sure to be a handful for England.

Carling himself was neither fazed nor over-confident about the challenge which lay ahead of him; neither was he about to launch into any radical strategy of captaincy in a bid to motivate his men.

'I'm just very honoured by it all,' he said. 'There is a lot of experience in the squad so it will be a question of gelling the side. We want cohesion and understanding between the two units, forwards and backs. It's for me to help plan the overall picture. It's given me a lot of confidence to be named for the season. I hope I can instil some of that into the team.'

Débutant Paul Ackford soars above the Australian line-out jumpers. At the age of 30, it was a remarkable change in fortune for Ackford, nine years after representing England B; he would go on to form a formidable second-row pairing with Wade Dooley.

There were seven changes in all from the side which had beaten Fiji 25–12 at the tail end of the Australian tour. Richard Harding, Gareth Chilcott, Barrie Evans, Bryan Barley, Stuart Barnes, Nigel Redman and Gary Rees were all casualties.

If the build-up was understated, with Carling taking time to ask the senior players for their views, the event itself was explosive. England played with rare passion, zeal, nerve and intelligence. The Twickenham crowd, so used to having their expectations thwarted, rose to applaud an invigorating performance as England ran out 28–19 winners. It's tempting to think that there were many nuggets of sporting truth, piercing insights, moments of revelation, passed on to the team by Cooke and Carling. The truth is always more mundane than romantic speculation might suggest. What can't be denied is that the sense of self-belief and purpose expressed by Cooke and tangibly displayed in his choice of Carling as captain and of the team itself, seeped deep into the bones of the squad. They played as if they meant it.

Australia in fact led twice, once after Leeds took advantage of a decoy run by Campese to touch down for a simple try by the posts, and then again, potentially more

ABOVE: Dewi Morris dives over the line to score on his international début and complete an impressive first game. Australian captain Nick Farr-Jones later praised Morris's performance at the post-match banquet.
BELOW: Rory Underwood wriggles into the corner to score the second of his two tries in a six-minute burst which helped to ensure an English victory over the Wallabies.

damaging, early in the second half when Campese intercepted a Webb pass intended for Halliday and sprinted sixty yards to score. That try put Australia clear at 13–9, the sides having turned round level at the interval. In other times at this point, on the receiving end of an unexpected score, England might have faltered, unsure of their own capabilities – not this time. They blazed back. Morris, who had been a scampering threat all afternoon, got on the scoresheet with a début try, Robinson charging down Lynagh's kick. Morris was singled out for praise by his opposite number, Australian captain Nick Farr-Jones, at the post-match banquet. It was Rory Underwood who dealt the real hammer blow to the Australians. He scored two tries within six minutes. The first came courtesy of Andrew, who had a commanding game in his twenty-first international. The second owed everything to the deft handling of Richards, Egerton, Moore and, finally, Robinson, whose beautiful pass cut out two defenders and put Underwood in at the corner.

Australia came back. ACT centre Girvan, in his first international, broke clear to create the overlap from which Grant scored. The score now stood at 22–19. Fittingly, though, it was Carling who provided the final narrative turn of a memorable afternoon. As the clock ticked on he made a decisive break and put Halliday clear to the line for his first try for England. Carling was heavily tackled in the move and was led from the field concussed. In fact, he had to be dragged off by England physio Kevin Murphy. The RFU doctor, Ben Gilfeather, stepped in to lend a supporting hand. John Buckton of Saracens came on to win his first cap.

'He took a knock earlier but he was fine and I let him carry on,' said Gilfeather. 'This time, although he was not unconscious, he was dazed and staggering and I didn't want him to carry on because he had been down twice in such a short time.'

England physio Kevin Murphy and RFU doctor Ben Gilfeather check out a dazed Will Carling during the match against Australia.

Dewi Morris and Brian Moore cross the line together as England score their first try against Ireland. Moore was later credited with the score.

Dean Richards was at the forefront of an impressive display by the English pack in Dublin, rounding off a fine afternoon by scoring England's second try.

As quickly as the cloud descended it lifted a fortnight later in Dublin. England faced down the passion of the Lansdowne Road crowd and the fury of the opposition to win 16–3. The pack, with Dooley and Ackford to the fore, were dominant. Behind them the doughty lieutenants, Richards and Teague, kept everyone in order. Andrew's two penalties put England 6–0 clear at the interval but he was having a difficult day with the boot. As a result, when the chance came in the second half to kick for goal, Carling opted to take a tap penalty. The forwards drove, Morris and Moore spiralled off the maul and over the line. Moore was later credited with the score. There was no squabbling over the second try-scorer, Richards making a typical charge over the line after good build-up from first Chris Oti and then Moore and Morris again. The English celebrated that night in Dublin, and no one more so than the captain. As he later commented in his biography, he learnt more off the field that day than on it.

> I got absolutely hammered at the dinner that night. A few days later Rob Andrew said to me that the lads were really surprised at my behaviour on Saturday night. It was a hell of a shock, probably bigger than being made captain. I was expected to behave in a certain way. That was a terrible realization for one so young. To have all those old guys expecting that. I couldn't be one of the boys any more.

To Carling's credit, his whole tenure of captaincy was marked by his ability to learn from mistakes. He had weaknesses he himself admitted. Like us all, it took some time before he recognized them. When he did, he was prepared to act, not necessarily to change but at least to ponder the position. To many it might seem as if the senior England citizens were being hypocritical killjoys – maybe they were – but if it mattered to them it mattered to Will Carling. He is not a great one for alcohol in any case. I personally never saw him drunk thereafter.

The season continued with its peaks and troughs. A tight, disciplined, wholehearted, collective performance accounted for the French, 11–0, on 4 March at Twickenham, thwarting France's own Grand Slam aspirations as well as laying down significant pointers to the type of rugby which England were to play over the coming years. Their pack took control and their discipline never wavered. Carling himself had the undeniable pleasure of his first international try, albeit one whose origins were rather messy. A planned England move was badly executed, leaving Carling holding the baby as all around shot off in unexpected directions.

Will Carling dives over the line to score his first international try, much to the delight of the Twickenham crowd. England won the game 11–0.

ABOVE: Tempers flare as Serge Blanco makes his point to referee Stephen Hilditch.
RIGHT: Dewi Morris and Rob Andrew celebrate England's victory over France.

Carling had the presence of mind to think on the hoof. He spotted that all the French markers were flummoxed as well, saw the gap and went through it to score. Robinson plunged over later to confirm England's impressive, if gradual, rise up the European rankings.

A fortnight later England suffered familiar grief in Cardiff. Once again they failed to handle the pressure of expectation. True, they were badly hampered right at the kick-off when Mike Teague was taken out of the game. It

was their nerve rather than their ability which was found wanting, a deficiency which was to cost them in dramatic fashion a year later at Murrayfield. Wales played with classic *hwyl*, ripping into England. Robert Jones turned the screw in the second half with his immaculate box-kicking. Wales, perhaps fortunate with Hall's try, nonetheless deserved their 12–9 win.

It was a sobering experience for the England camp. At the first severe test of Carling's captaincy, he didn't pass muster.

'We never got to grips with the problems,' said Roger Uttley. 'We were up for the championship yet we couldn't handle it. We simply couldn't work our way past our difficulties.'

There was still one game to go, against Romania, and a Lions party to aim for, but Carling's body thought differently. The pain from the shin splints was now too

Robert Jones proved to be Wales's playmaker. He took control around the base of the scrum as Wales went on to win 12–9.

great to ignore. Medical tests eventually revealed a stress fracture of the lower left fibia. Carling was selected for the British Lions but was forced to withdraw; also from the England team to play Romania in Bucharest. An unknown, Jeremy Guscott, took his place. Guscott was not to remain in the shadows for very long; and that suited Will Carling just fine.

Jeremy Guscott scored three tries in his sensational début match for England against Romania.

Chapter Two

1989–90:
England meet their maker

A Lions tour can break as well as make a reputation. That little truth was to come home to Will Carling four years later in New Zealand when he had a traumatic time, though he rallied and proved that he is no soft touch.

Of course, wisdom and insight only ever arrive when it's too late. If only someone could get hindsight to turn up in advance on occasions. As it was, in September 1989, Will Carling might well have felt a little bit out in the cold, perhaps a touch regretful that he had missed the Lions trip to Australia that summer. Maybe there was even a twinge of envy in there at the acclaim showered on his team-mates who had turned round a losing series to see off the Australian challenge. Those who sniffed at the achievement, damning Australia as unworthy of a full Lions tour, had to eat their words a couple of years later as the Wallabies swept all before them in the World Cup.

Several England players returned from the Lions tour in huge credit. The Lions pack might almost have been clothed in white. Paul Ackford, Wade Dooley, Brian Moore, Dean Richards and, the player of the series, Mike Teague, had grown in stature almost by the minute through the tour, a fierce, tight-knit, unyielding gang who marched side by side towards the noise of the guns. Jeremy Guscott, that unknown lad from Bath, Carling's replacement and a wild selectorial gamble, was now a fixture in any side. His class, his temperament, his obvious relish for the big occasion (who can ever forget that audacious grubber kick and gather for the decisive try in the second Test?) induced a warm glow in every England supporter contemplating the forthcoming season.

But above all it was Rob Andrew who returned home with his ratings enhanced. He had gone to Australia as third-choice fly half, an early replacement for the injured Paul Dean of Ireland. Andrew clutched the opportunity to his breast and refused to let it go. By the end of the tour

the occasionally hesitant, unsure, wayward Andrew had blossomed into the man of calm and control who was to direct England with such authority over the next half dozen years. The great irony was that the coach who helped him find himself, who brought all the latent talent to the surface, was Ian McGeechan, the same man who coached the opposition six months later at Murrayfield – one of the delicious retrospective reflections on what turned out to be an astonishing season.

For the moment, though, as the English players limbered up for the third season of competitive league rugby, thoughts were only of building on the foundations of the previous year. If Will Carling did harbour any jealous thoughts about the success of his colleagues, they were no more than the laudable instincts of any sportsman to perform at the highest level. Carling, in fact, was just happy to be rid of the aggravation from his shin which had so plagued him the previous year. He entered the season in confident mood, buoyed by the relative success of the preceding year and relishing the prospect of developing his captaincy skills. He had done everything off the cuff the year before. This is not to say that he was unprepared, only that he had no precedent, no point of reference, on which to base his approach. He had no means of calibrating his performance other than against the scoreboard at the end of the game. This time around, with more time to plan, more experience under the belt, he could take a more considered view of events.

There were some adjustments to make to his life as well. On the sporting front he switched from playing for the North to London. Rob Andrew made a similar decision. They took some stick for it but the demands of training and travelling, the increased club commitments, made it impossible to keep the old allegiances. It was a sign of things to come. The changing rugby landscape swept away so many of the old traditions and loyalties. The players were not to blame for this. The situation was

forced upon them and they merely reacted to it. Many people conveniently forgot this over the coming months and years as they targeted Carling for his so-called selfish, commercially triggered attitude. It was during the course of this year that the England captain left Mobil to set up his own promotional and marketing company, Inspirational Horizons.

Money and sport move ever closer. Carling, unlike many others, never lost sight of the relationship between the two. If you sidelined the latter in pursuit of the

seriously and, in so doing, took his eye of his obligations to his club, Harlequins. Even though Cooke had granted Carling the luxury of long-term support, the player himself knew it would only last if his form endured. Besides, there was personal pride at stake. So Carling saw the emergence of Guscott on the scene as a spur, as an incentive to get fitter, faster and stronger.

'I realize I have to prove I'm fit again and that I'm playing to the required standard,' said Carling. 'If I'm not, I would have no desire to hold on to my place. Last

![Rugby match photograph]

Mark Linnett, winning his only cap, scores one of England's ten tries in their match against Fiji .Rory Underwood scored five tries, which made him England's joint top try scorer of all time.

former, you would invariably end up with neither. Carling took his sport and, in particular, the England captaincy very seriously. Indeed there were to be times when he perhaps took his England responsibilities too

season was tough both mentally and physically and by the end of it I was shattered. I went through the season on one good leg: two legs should make quite a difference.'

Carling's determination to prove himself a player of substance and to take nothing for granted found an echo in the early season comments of Geoff Cooke. His end-of-year report on Carling had been favourable; so were his views now.

'We made a very positive decision when we appointed Will and obviously we would want to see that through,' said Cooke. 'He made an excellent start last year. He suffered because of his injury problems but he still made a major contribution. He gained the respect of his fellow players. To justify our confidence, Will always has to perform as a player, but that was always understood between us. It's not a sinecure but there would have to be a fairly dramatic and disastrous loss of form to be thinking of changing at this stage.'

exciting newcomer had not been given first shout. So began the long relationship between Will Carling and Jeremy Guscott, one which promised so much and which flourished initially in brilliant fashion.

In a sparky encounter at Twickenham, Fiji were seen off 58–23. Rory Underwood scored five tries for England to equal the record of Dan Lambert for a single match and also to nudge alongside Cyril Lowe's career record of eighteen tries. This was no carnival romp, however. It was a brutally fought match during which the Fijians

Even though there was speculation in the press that the Bath club pairing of Simon Halliday and Jeremy Guscott might be preferred for the November international against Fiji, there was never any real danger of it coming to pass. The real choice was between Halliday and Guscott. After Guscott's dramatic introduction to Test rugby (he scored a hat-trick on his début against Romania) there would have been a public outcry if the

Mickey Skinner battles his way through the Fijian defence during England's bruising 58–23 victory.

completely lost their cool. Two of their threequarters, Tevita Vonolagi and Noa Nadruku, were sent off. A couple of their team-mates were lucky to stay on the field as they went hunting for heads rather than legs in the tackle.

Wounded in battle, Jeff Probyn shows the scars. The English pack, however, were starting to show their complete supremacy over each of their opponents.

Brian Moore lends a hand as Simon Hodgkinson tries to come to terms with the near-impossible kicking conditions in the Parc des Princes. Despite this, Hodgkinson contributed four penalties and a conversion as England ran out 26–7 winners – their biggest margin of victory in seventy years.

MAIN PICTURE: Jeremy Guscott takes advantage of a French defensive error to win the race for the line ahead of French winger Patrice Lagisquet.

INSET: Listen up! Will Carling offers his advice to the senior members of the side.

impressed. They might have been playing in black shirts adorned with a silver fern so commanding was their play. They faced down their opponents and the French froze as a result. It took France many years to overcome the trauma of this defeat, spooked by English mind games as much as their play on the day.

Despite the vicious wind which swirled round the ground Simon Hodgkinson was on song. His three early penalties set up the platform. England led 13–0 at the break, their other points coming after a beautifully weighted blindside grubber had enabled Underwood to scoot past the dozing defence and score. Guscott took

advantage of Charvet's fluffed chip kick to gather and race to the line. The climax, though, belonged to Carling who fixed Blanco with a sidestep and devastating burst of acceleration. This was England's biggest margin of victory here in over seventy years. These were bright times for England.

'We're getting there,' said Carling. 'But there really is much more.'

Richard Hill's sniping runs from the base of the scrum, coupled with his quick service, proved to be decisive factors in England's 34–6 victory against Wales which set up a Grand Slam decider with Scotland.

The England captain brushes off the Welsh defence to complete a memorable solo try during England's controlled and impressive victory over Wales.

England were on something of a roll and facing a sequence of three consecutive victories in the championship for the first time in a decade. Caution was once again the watchword. It must have been difficult to apply the brakes because England were flying and everyone knew it – even the Welsh.

There were some who pretended that Wales might once again put the evil eye on English aspiration but even these diehards could not deny the evidence of their own eyes. There was no anti-climax at Twickenham a fortnight later as England ran out winners by 34–6. The English pack was in a league of its own while Richard Hill's slick, speedy service from scrum half launched wave after wave of attacks. Carling led the way with a superb solo try after just five minutes, threading his way past tacklers, handing off those who did manage to get a finger near him to dive in at the corner. Underwood scored tries either side of the interval, the second a long seventy-five-yard sprint to the line after an interception. Hill also got his name on the scoresheet.

It was the overall impression, though, rather than the mere detail of the scores which made such an impact. Here was a team in total control, full of positive intention, deep self-belief, secure in the knowledge that they could play any sort of game. The forwards were not just a solid lump. Against Wales they blazed around the field parading their fitness and their footballing abilities. The backs, meanwhile, were taking full advantage, rattling up tries at an unprecedented rate. No, nothing could stop this lot.

And then came Murrayfield.

How that long, slow walk by David Sole must stalk the dreams of the England players. The game was lost for many other reasons, of course, but somehow the staged entrance captured the mood of the day. It spoke of Scottish resolve, pride, history and resistance. Bannockburn, Culloden, the poll tax, English imperialism; they were all in there somewhere. It was not so much that any of this deeply affected the precise individual performance of the Scottish players. What it affected was the crowd. Ian McGeechan still talks of the moment when he first heard that rumbling noise which signalled the start of the swelling roar. McGeechan was under the stand at the time, on his way to his seat, yet he knew in that instant that something special and dramatic was afoot. Rugby is a game of the emotions every bit as much as it is a game of technical skill. If there is no passion, no commitment, the skills will be swamped. Of course, this does not mean that players run around like demented wildebeest. Their emotion needs control and refinement. There is no doubt, though, that the support of the Murrayfield crowd had a major impact on proceedings. It lifted the Scots and, in so doing, fazed the English. The runaway train came off the track in spectacular fashion.

The build-up had been smooth. England had a month off after their stunning brace of wins over France and Wales. Some might argue that the extended break caused them to lose momentum. Such theories, whichever way they are worked, are invariably nonsense. You could argue with equal merit that they came into the match refreshed and better prepared. That England were overwhelming favourites to take the Grand Slam (plus every other trophy, real or mythical, from Calcutta Cup to Triple Crown) was not due to overbearing arrogance on the part of the team nor blinkered delusion on the part of the English press. The press called the match as logic dictated. England were in superb form, Scotland were not. They had scuffed their way to three victories, showing some character but no great skill. They had scraped home 13–10 in a halting match in Dublin, eventually took control against France after Alain Carminati was sent off for stamping on John Jeffrey, and were let off the hook in Cardiff, where Wales failed to take their chances, enabling Scotland to sneak home 13–9.

Scotland did have one priceless asset however – coach Ian McGeechan. Not only was he able to offer a sure touch to his own men, he also knew the opposition backwards, having coached so many of them with the Lions less than a year before. It was quite in order that one newspaper should strike a wonderful headline over a match preview: 'England Prepare to Meet Their Maker'.

McGeechan left no stone unturned in preparing his men to face England. Every night in the two weeks building up to the match McGeechan would lead his

MAIN PICTURE: Tony Stanger, Chris Gray and the whole of Scotland celebrate the Scots' crucial try just into the start of the second half.
INSET: Jeremy Guscott crosses the line to give England the lead during the titanic Grand Slam encounter at Murrayfield.

So near yet so far. The English pack is held up just short of the line in the desperate last minutes of the match at Murrayfield. Try as they might, England could not cross the line as the Scots hung on for a historic victory.

normal family life at home in Leeds and then, as others headed for bed, he would head for the video. Far into the night he would search the tapes looking for weaknesses in the opposition and devising ways to maximize the strengths of this own players. McGeechan's simple contention was that his team would have to view England as once they viewed the French.

'We knew that if things were done badly, then you could safely assume that they would score,' said McGeechan. 'If we gave England too much space they would exploit it and we would be out of the game. It was as clear-cut as that.'

A few hundred miles to the south, England's preparations were also going well; in retrospect, maybe too well.

'Everyone is ready,' said Carling. 'We have the confidence that comes from an established pattern and there is a mood of calmness among the players.'

Many England players felt that their Friday training session was one of the best they had ever had. It was slick, ordered and damn near perfect. There wasn't a pass dropped in the entire forty-five minutes. Maybe if England had fluffed that final training session, spilled a few passes, grumbled a bit, set each other on edge, then they might have gone into the match with that crucial bit of fear in their mind. Who's to say? There is no such thing as the perfect preparation; only the perfect result. England didn't get it.

The match was a watershed in Carling's career. Scotland's 13–7 victory made front page news across the land. The atmosphere on the day, and the intensity of the game itself, will linger forever in the minds of those who were there. For Carling, and several of the senior players, the haunting memory was to have a significant impact on the style of rugby England were to play over the next eighteen months. For the captain, the defeat was to be a huge blot on his record; not so much for the loss in itself but for the manner of it.

England had several chances to score points through

the boot of Simon Hodgkinson. Time and again they opted instead for a scrum to try and shove the Scots back over their line. The ploy was a failure. If Hodgkinson had been out of touch all season, there might just have been some mileage in England's approach; but he hadn't. There had been a fierce wind blowing at Parc des Princes, as there was here at Murrayfield, but Hodgkinson had delivered. England succumbed to hubris, believing the power of their own publicity. Of course they could shunt the Scots scrummage backwards. Hadn't they got the core of the British Lions pack? Sport, mercifully, rarely listens to logic's pleadings. Scotland, through buckling, twisting, dropping, held their scrum. It was 9–4 at the interval, Guscott having scored a lovely try. Craig Chalmers kicked three goals. But the fact that England hadn't taken advantage of their superiority was obviously preying on nerves. England made a desperate sequence of mistakes at the start of the second half, Scotland pounced, Tony Stanger scored an opportunist try and it was virtually all over.

Carling took a roasting. England were accused of being arrogant, assuming that victory was there for the taking, and the captain was rebuked for letting the forwards, particularly Brian Moore, hijack decision-making.

'I'm aware that a lot of people thought that I made a mistake,' said Carling a few months later. 'I still reckon we could have scored a pushover try from that position near the line. If we had done, it would have been a massive psychological boost, far greater than scoring a penalty. I still think it was worth taking the risk.'

The dressing-room was a desolate place. All the players were emotionally shattered. It was a sight which affected Carling deeply. However, the real magnitude of the defeat probably only really hit home in subsequent years. Time and time again he was pestered, in bars, restaurants and even in the street by people wanting to know why he had run those penalties. Finally, in his biography, Carling himself admitted his deficiency.

'At Murrayfield I didn't assert myself enough,' he said.

How ironic that there were times in the coming eighteen months when he was to assert himself in ways not to everyone's liking. Carling was about to enter some very turbulent waters.

Chapter Three

1990–91:
Grand Slam shoot-out – part two

It had all seemed so easy. Good-looking public schoolboy from military background becomes youngest England captain for over half a century and immediately the national side win matches as well as friends with their emphatic, positive rugby. The boy done good, as they say in other arenas. Carling, and England, looked destined for great things.

The Murrayfield defeat, however, was a defining moment. It proved that Carling had feet of clay, that the fault-line of under-achievement which had run through English rugby for so many decades was still there and that sport could not be played as if it were a computer programme in which the outcome is forever predictable. Perhaps Will Carling is able to look back on that day and appreciate that adversity can shape and enhance a character far more than mere success. For the moment,

of these problems he brought upon himself; others were imposed upon him by the arcane, occasionally hypocritical ways of the RFU, an institution uneasy about the direction in which the amateur game was moving.

Carling first had to contend with more failure on the playing field. The late summer tour to Argentina was a disaster. None of the management appeared to want the trip. Many of the players certainly did not. Several of the old hands announced their unavailability. There was no Guscott, no Andrew, no Ackford, Richards, Teague or Rory Underwood. In all there were fourteen uncapped players in the squad. Those who did go had concerns at the back of their minds that they would be on the rugby road virtually all the way through to the end of the World Cup in November 1991. Carling himself, though, saw the tour in a positive light.

though, his morale and confidence were about to take a severe buffeting, the end result of which was that he almost walked away from the England captaincy. Some

Nigel Heslop and David Pears are pressurized during the first Test against Argentina in Buenos Aires. England were victorious but went on to lose the second Test one week later.

own inclination, was becoming more and more widely known. He was straying from the usual muddied-oaf territory of the back pages on to showbusiness, glossy feature turf. There were colour spreads of him in a variety of magazines. There was nothing intrinsically wrong or untoward in all this. Some of his later critics, notably Jeff Probyn, suggested that Carling was making mileage out of his position, one which would have no standing if it weren't for the sweaty efforts of Probyn and his mates. Probyn sensed a build-up of resentment from all this, particularly as Carling was at the time working to establish his own marketing company and any publicity was good publicity.

It was not just Probyn who took exception to Carling's increasingly high profile. Within the RFU there was a significant faction who wanted to clip the wings of the darling of the gossip columns. Carling was twice called upon to explain the financial arrangements behind a couple of public appearances he had made, one of which was a routine modelling assignment for *You* magazine. Elsewhere someone had faxed the RFU a copy of an invoice alleging that Carling was to receive money for opening a leisure centre. The sums of money involved were minimal and, in any case, had been passed on to charity.

The small detail of these matters is so trivial as not to be worthy of consideration. However, the manner in which Carling was hauled over the coals was hugely significant. It encapsulated the discomfort of the RFU with the direction in which the game was heading: in essence these incidents expressed their deep-rooted objection to professionalism and all it entailed more truthfully than any laborious paper they might have put out on the matter. They are still at war with their hearts and minds today. Above all else, their treatment of Carling smacked of hypocrisy.

When he was appointed in 1988, one of the many things in his favour was that he would be a good role model for the game. He was young and approachable, a PR man's delight. The RFU expressly wanted someone to market the game on their behalf, to project the game to a wider audience, particularly to those who might in other

Jason Leonard and Pedro Sporleder square up during the ill-tempered match at Twickenham which saw the dismissal of Féderico Mendez following an unseemly swipe at Paul Ackford.

times have played the game in state schools but who no longer had access to the sport. As well as this, the RFU were bent on making the national team more competitive, and their own domestic structure harder-edged through official leagues. The England team itself was designated as the shop window for the sport. Carling, along with Geoff Cooke, was charged with delivering all of this. When he did, they hammered him for it.

'I'm getting seriously tired of having to go through this kind of thing,' said Carling. 'If I wanted to be payed for playing, I would go north. I knew the regulations as they stood and I was not going to be stupid enough to lose my amateur status for £200 or £300.'

Carling had battles to fight on other fronts. Some Harlequin members were unhappy with the level of his commitment to the club. Who was right and who was wrong depended on which end of the spectrum you favoured. Carling had never made any secret of the fact that he regarded England as his primary concern. Other players, notably those at Bath, would never dream of less than total allegiance to the club first.

What was really at issue in all this was Carling's image. He was seen as aloof, selfish and arrogant, concerned only with furthering his own interests, on and off the pitch. He appeared to be above the menial chores and duties which most club players had to put up with. There was a blurring between appearance and reality in all this carping. It's doubtful if Carling himself would claim to be the ultimate club man. Yet he did have pressures unique to his position of England captain, some of which, admittedly, he generated himself. However Dick Best, then coach at Quins, a former player and long-standing member and a man not dedicated to setting up a welfare state for players, has always had sympathy for Carling's position even if, as we shall see, he did not always agree with it.

So much for the background and the mitigating circumstances. Carling did not ride the choppy waters too well. In December, hard on the heels of the other problems, came a fall-out with the London Division. Carling missed the opening match through injury but was due to return the following week. He missed the midweek

training session after being delayed on business in Scotland, but rather than phone the London chairman of selectors, Graham Smith, to let him know, Carling rang Rob Andrew instead and asked him to pass on the news. London, whose coach was Best, were not impressed and Carling was dropped.

The pre-Christmas stretch had proved to be a bumpy ride (Carling was also in hot water for remarks he made about Paul Gascoigne). He was in the doldrums and was within a whisker of giving up the captaincy. He phoned Rob Andrew to tell him that he was seriously thinking of doing so. Andrew talked him round, England went off to a New Year training camp in Lanzarote and returned to win a Grand Slam. The fickle mistress that is sport!

If those difficult few months served to add a bit of steel to Carling's character, it stood him in good stead for facing the Cardiff bogey yet again. In mid-January England, like so many of their predecessors, set off on the short journey across the border knowing that if everything went to form they would win. This time they did. The Lanzarote camp had helped to forge a collective cussedness, a desire to set the record books straight after the Murrayfield mishap the previous year. The team changed the routine which had served them so abysmally down the long barren stretch of twenty-eight years since their last win in Cardiff. Instead of staying out in the secluded comfort of Chepstow, where the quiet could prey upon taut nerves, Geoff Cooke took them right into the heart of Cardiff city centre. They could see the Arms Park from the hotel windows. Cooke had also handed out tapes of the Welsh songs so as to acclimatize the players. By the end of the afternoon of 19 January it was difficult to recall what all the fuss had been about. England had won easily, 25–6, with a try from Mike Teague and a world record seven penalties from Simon Hodgkinson. England, in stark contrast to their previous championship campaign, were cautious and conservative, but no one could blame them for that.

In fact, no one had a chance, for England refused all TV and press interviews after the match. It was an extraordinary collective decision by the England camp, one which created a huge storm of protest and took the

ABOVE: Mike Teague dives over the line to score England's only try of their 25–6 victory over Wales which ended their twenty-eight-year losing stretch in Cardiff. OPPOSITE: Dean Richards picks up from the back of the scrum to attack the Welsh defence. Mark Ring waits in anticipation.

gloss completely off their historic victory. If for no other reason than that their motives for withdrawing from the press conferences were subsequently misrepresented, the squad were woefully misguided in their actions. It was said that they were demanding money for interviews from the BBC and when it was not forthcoming they went into purdah.

The truth of the matter was more complex, less sinister but, nonetheless, utterly ridiculous. The players were now allowed a certain latitude in earning money from off-field commercial activities. God bless the RFU, what ought to have been simple guidelines were instead clouded with grey areas. The players set up a company called Player Vision and entered into an arrangement

with a company run by former England cricketer Bob Willis. It was Willis who had made a request to the BBC for a £5,000 facility interview fee. Nothing happened until the week of the match itself when the BBC raised the matter with the RFU. They in turn stated that under the normal regulations for England get-togethers the squad should be available for interview free of charge. The players decided, therefore, not to give interviews to the BBC until the matter was resolved.

This was only one area of friction. The players had also been unhappy with the level of press demands on their time. They wanted some boundaries mapped out so that they would not be pestered from dawn to dusk for interviews. It was a justifiable grievance, but Cardiff Arms Park was not the place to bring it to a head.

Finally Geoff Cooke thought that they were being hassled in their moment of victory and simply wanted a few more minutes breathing space; or so he said. There was an awful lot of rumour and half-truth flying about

that day. So they boycotted all press conferences. It was a cack-handed and naive protest, unworthy of sixth-form schoolboys, let alone international sportsmen. Geoff Cooke admitted as much quite openly later. He got it completely wrong. Cooke wasn't saying this just to save his own skin. He was to repeat it many times in private conversation. There was a need to save his skin, though, because the RFU was incensed. Even though Carling had been heavily to the fore in leading the walk-out, Cooke took the heat. It took some nimble-footed diplomacy from RFU president Mike Pearey to hold off the hawks who wanted the heads of both Cooke and Carling. They both survived.

Carling has never been wholly at ease with the press. Perhaps it is impossible to be so. Certainly he would have reflected ruefully on how tame the rugby press actually were a few years later when the so-called Rottweilers from the tabloids got stuck into him (and his dustbins) following his alleged affair with Princess Diana. Carling, though, has always been approachable and, by and large, obliging. Of course there are times when there is friction. It's inevitable given that the press are there to criticize

performance, for better or worse. For the most part Carling has endured all the press conferences, during which he is often asked endless variations on the same basic question, with courteous stoicism. He gets on well with some journalists; not so well with others. This is normal run-of-the-mill interaction between any group of people.

At this point in his career, he felt he was getting a hard time of it. He wasn't. It just felt that way. One of his failings, or perhaps we should say traits, is that he has always bruised more easily than some when there is criticism flying around. The anxieties were not over for this season, but Carling could afford to shrug them off. The team was on its way to a Grand Slam.

Scotland were next up. England had a month's break, most of which time was spent in endless discussion about what the players might and might not be allowed to do in terms of their off-field earnings. The severe weather hampered the build-up. The Scots travelled south with a defeat in Paris (15–9) and a crushing victory over Wales (32–12) behind them. It was a different scene at Twickenham, now such an intimidating venue for opposition teams. Once again England took the percentage route, relying on their forwards to secure the ball and wrap up the game. Hodgkinson's boot swung deadly as ever for his seventeen points from five penalties and a conversion of Heslop's try. The final margin was 21–12 in England's favour and it was off to Dublin for the Triple Crown.

No side travels to Lansdowne Road easy in heart. They appreciate the hospitality but dread the welcome committee on the pitch. In this case their sense of

LEFT: The might of the England pack was proving to be too much of a force for any side during the 1991 championship.
OPPOSITE PAGE
MAIN PICTURE: Could David Sole summon up the passion from his side to repeat the performance that gave Scotland the Grand Slam in 1990?
INSET TOP: Nigel Heslop beats Alex Moore over the line to score the only try of the game for England.
INSET BOTTOM: Yet again the boot of Simon Hodgkinson proved lethal as he notched up 17 points during the 21–12 victory over Scotland.

ABOVE: Simon Geoghegan dives into the corner to cause England some angst at Lansdowne Road. BELOW: Rory Underwood, England's supreme finisher, makes the game and the Triple Crown safe for England as they beat Ireland 16–7. Next stop Twickenham and France for the Grand Slam decider.

foreboding proved accurate. This was England's toughest match of all. If it hadn't been for the intervention of Dean Richards in the last quarter, during which Rory Underwood finally settled matters with a clinical bout of finishing, England's dreams might have perished. But on they went, 16–7 winners.

For the second season in a row, it all came down to the last match, this time a Grand Slam shoot-out against France. England were unchanged throughout the championship, a remarkable feat when you cast your mind back to the topsy-turvy pre-Carling era. It was only the second time ever they had managed to remain so. France, true to tradition and folklore, were the romantic's favourites. They had scored six tries in hammering Wales 36–3 just a fortnight earlier. England, in contrast, were steady, efficient and dependable. The pack would draw the sting from unruly opposition, Hodgkinson would exact due revenge from any infringements and then, but only then, might England let the ball go. You could argue

Will Carling, Jeremy Guscott and Rory Underwood celebrate the latter's opening try for England. Despite the French scoring three tries to England's one, England were victorious by 21–19 to win the Grand Slam.

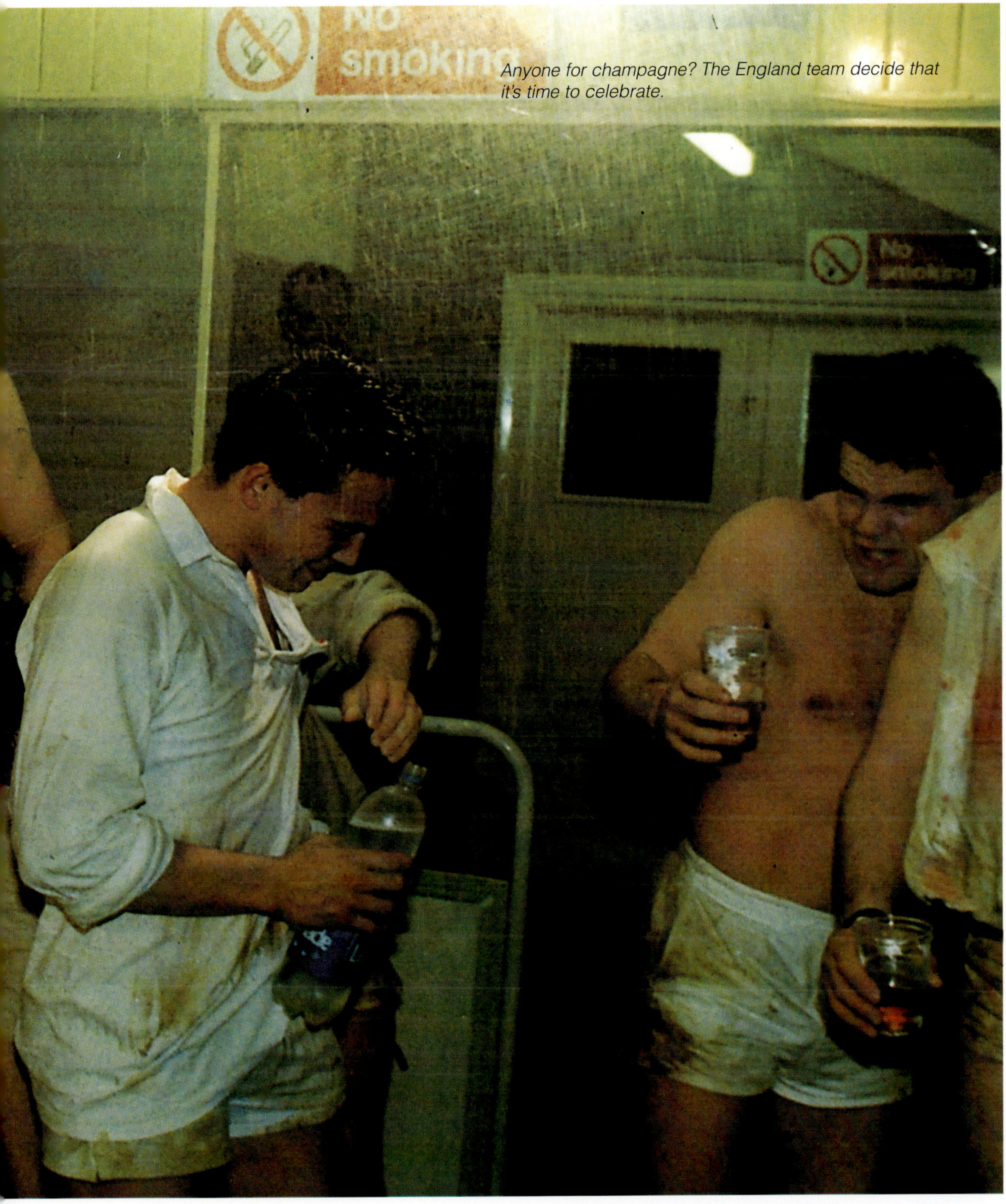

Anyone for champagne? The England team decide that it's time to celebrate.

– and the columns of the national press were full of such arguments – that England were one-eyed, limited and wasting the massive talent they had outside. All this is true but after the trauma of Murrayfield 1990 they were, for this season at least, justified in playing it tight.

They had to draw on every last drop of their resolve and control against France. It was a tumultuous Twickenham day. The English pack put in a Herculean effort and France scored perhaps the greatest try ever seen in the championship. France outscored England by three tries to one but England deserved their 21–19 victory for the precise direction of Hill and Andrew at half back and the sheer power and will of their pack.

France had Saint-André's try to savour. The move began behind France's posts, Camberabero sweeping down the right wing before chip-kicking across where his team-mate gathered and scored. England, though had a deeper pleasure. At long last, and for only the second time in thirty-four years, they had a Grand Slam to their name. It had been Will Carling's most difficult season to date. It had also been his most satisfying.

Will Carling, the first Grand Slam-winning captain since Bill Beaumont in 1980, leaves the field to start the serious celebrations with his side.

Chapter Four

1991–92:
England fall at the final hurdle in the World Cup

There was little time for Carling or for England to draw breath after their Grand Slam success. There was the usual frantic end to the club season to contend with. Carling was involved for his club in the Pilkington Cup final against Northampton which they came perilously close to losing. They only finally saw off the robust challenge of the Saints in extra time, 25–13.

For all the excitement of the playing challenges – the prospect of a summer tour to Australia and the World Cup, to be played in Britain, Ireland and France, steaming up rapidly on the horizon – Will Carling had plenty of sobering thoughts to occupy his summer months. He knew that he would have to pace himself if he were to sustain his form and his enthusiasm in what

was going to be the busiest period of his rugby life. There was a more chilling reality to contend with, one which had struck home during the previous season: one more slip and he would be sacked.

'I seriously wonder how long I will continue to play because of the pressures,' Carling had said during those traumatic months when his captaincy was under intense scrutiny. 'I realize that at the age of 25 it is an amazing thing to say, but it may be that I have only one year left in me. Everything that is happening round the sport is burning people out. I didn't ask for a high profile. I didn't

Tim Gavin and Simon Poidevin trample over Mike Teague as Australia give the English pack a lesson in power and mobility during their 40–15 victory.

MAIN PICTURE: Tim Gavin congratulates Willie
Ofahengaue on the first of his two tries.
INSET: The Australian team celebrate their convincing
victory.

ask to be made captain at 22. Of course it would be smug of me to carp about it all when I know that I'm lucky to be captain.'

There was no easing up of pressure. The tour to Australia was seen in some quarters as foolhardy, a ludicrous strain on already tired bodies. The management saw it as a chance to keep the clock ticking and to force the players to confront the realities of the opposition they were to face for higher stakes in the World Cup just a few months hence. As it was, England struggled to find any sort of form, losing three of the seven matches. They crashed badly in the Test against Australia, going down 40–15. As ever, some reputations were made – Martin Bayfield showed the potential of what was to come in later years – and, cruelly, some were lost. The hero of the Grand Slam, Simon Hodgkinson, who had scored a record 60 points during that campaign, fell from grace. He took a heavy blow to the face in one of the early tour

games and never regained his confidence. Jonathan Webb took full advantage, played in the Tests against Fiji and Australia, and never looked back.

For Australia there was the prospect of revenge over many of the England players who had tormented them in British Lions shirts just a couple of years earlier. The punishment was inflicted in no uncertain manner. The Test victory was a huge morale boost for the Australians and a personal triumph for their coach, Bob Dwyer. He masterminded the tactics which saw Australia attack England in what many in Britain had reckoned to be one of their strongest areas – the back row. The lack of defensive pace from the base of the scrum, particularly that of Richards, was exposed. A new star was introduced

to the world in the very large shape of Willie Ofahengaue. The young flanker scored two tries and No. 8 Tim Gavin dominated Richards as Australia ran in five tries. England scrabbled through the rubble for some consolation.

'At least it showed us what we will be up against in the World Cup,' said Roger Uttley. 'They out-thought us and were much faster round the field. But we now know exactly what we've got to do.'

The players had few illusions. They had known the draw for a long time and it did them few favours. They were to open the tournament by playing the defending champions, New Zealand. If that went to form, and the All Blacks won, then England would in all probability have to travel to Paris to face France in the quarter-final.

'We have the toughest draw of all,' said Carling. 'But then if you aspire to win a World Cup you have to beat all the best teams at some point. Luck comes into it because one penalty can decide a match. But if you're good enough and fit enough you make your own luck.'

Of course Carling was confident of England's own chances but he knew that in the shake-down between the leading countries – New Zealand, France, Australia and themselves – there would be little in it.

The World Cup was to be a watershed for the England rugby players. The profile of the game which was rising slowly but not dramatically suddenly shot off into orbit. Several of the players – Brian Moore, Jeremy Guscott, Rory Underwood – became household faces as well as names. Will Carling was glad of the company for he alone had laboured in the spotlight for the past few years.

As Brian Moore wrote in his autobiography:

> The World Cup was the advent of the celebrity status for the top England players. Now and again before the World Cup we might be recognized in the street. After the World Cup it was never the same again. People would recognize you all over the place, speak in stage whispers about you as you went by. It became impossible for Will to emerge in public without being besieged. For me, fame was not the best bit of being an international. It was the worst bit.

The fame came with a rush. The start of the season was a slow burner. England had arranged three warm-up games, against the USSR, Gloucester and England Students, all of which were won by comfortable margins, respectively 53–0, 34–4 and 35–0. The World Cup squad had been finalized (no Stuart Barnes, no John Hall and no

England took on USSR in a warm-up game for the World Cup winning comfortably – by 53–0.

Martin Bayfield), final fitness targets were being chased and the finer points of commercial deals were being put into place.

Part of the reason for the ambivalent attitude – or, in some quarters, downright hostility – people have towards Will Carling stems from the fact that for the last half dozen years or so his name has been associated with money. Every season there had been some new commercial development or some further nibbling away at the hidebound amateur regulations and every season Will Carling (along with Brian Moore) had been targeted as the driving force behind such moves. To many, Carling personified the new thrusting money-grabbing player. He was rugby's first yuppie, a Thatcherite in a white shirt. While it's true to say that Carling was indeed at the heart of most of these discussions, it's unfair to pillory him for it. He was the captain of the squad. Ever since his early days he had declared his hand in seeing himself as the players' representative, a conduit between the squad and the committee. It so happened that many of the progressive inclinations of the players chimed with Carling's own attitude. He too wanted a piece of the commercial action but only because everyone else was getting in on the act round the world. He saw it as right and proper. He wanted fair play off the field in the same way as he always played by the book on the field.

There's little doubt, given his background, that he would have made money somehow and somewhere in his life. It just so happened that his life was rugby and there were opportunities opening up. To portray him as some avaricious hooligan, bent only on lining his own pocket and destroying the old fabric, is a grievous distortion. He was no shrinking violet, of course, when it came to putting his case forward, but he could also be conciliatory and cautious. Brian Moore revealed in his autobiography that a few senior players actually contemplated going on

strike over the money disputes the previous season. Carling appeased the militants. They were angry at what they saw as deliberate foot-dragging and the hypocrisy of the RFU. The squad had agreed to advertise Timberland gear and an advert was duly placed in the Calcutta Cup programme. The ad met all the criteria laid down about players not wearing rugby kit. The RFU pulled the plug. Meanwhile the Scots and the Welsh were sanctioning such adverts. In the southern hemisphere the players just giggled at the old country getting her knickers in a twist over not very much. For the World Cup the England players, after a requisite amount of haggling and hair-splitting, agreed a deal entitled 'Run with the Ball' which involved several sponsors. The squad would give coaching clinics during the competition in return for money. By the end of the season they pulled in about £5,000 a man, hardly a king's ransom.

Carling's real focus was narrowing all the time, right down to the kick-off against New Zealand at Twickenham. It had been six years since England last faced the All Blacks. They lost both Tests on that tour. They fared little better here. The final score may have appeared close, 18–12, but the uncomfortable truth for England was that New Zealand appeared to have a good bit in reserve. It was a halting match, rigorously refereed by Scot Jim Fleming. Michael Jones, the peerless All Black flanker, scored the game's only try. The start had been an anti-climax for all concerned. The England captain put on a brave face.

'We lost control in the second half,' said Carling. 'I don't think we did ourselves justice.'

If there had ever been any doubt as to the magnitude of the task which lay before them, any lingering complacency that playing on home turf would tilt the scales in their favour, it was blown away by the defeat.

England were based out at Basingstoke. The squad travelled to Otley to watch their next opponents, Italy,

beat the USA 30–9. They learnt nothing. Italy were duly beaten at Twickenham by England, 36–6, as were the USA in the final pool match, 37–9, both very run-of-the-mill games.

'It was a convincing victory but not an impressive one,' said Rob Andrew of the American match.

As the knock-out stage was reached, the tournament was running to form. England were to travel to Paris to meet France in the quarter-final. In the USA match Carling had passed Bill Beaumont's record of captaining England twenty-one times but the landmark meant little at the time. The tournament was entering the white-knuckle zone as all that planning, all that sweaty labour, detailed preparation and feverish, excited anticipation, came down to an eighty-minute match. If it was lost, despite the immense difficulty of the task, England would be branded as failures.

England had a short break in Jersey before travelling to Paris. It was there that Geoff Cooke pondered the most difficult selection decision of his life. He was brave enough to back his rational assessment of the challenge England had to meet, even though he knew that if it backfired he would be for the chop. The bone-crunching, big-tackling Mick Skinner came in for Dean Richards, Cooke reasoning that the French needed to be cut down at source and that Deano's shortcomings around the fringes, which had been exposed on the Australian tour, might cost England dear. Even though Carling was consulted on selection matters, his influence on such a key decision was minimal. It was Cooke's call. Some players took exception to the captain being so closely involved, reasoning that he had been guaranteed his place and so had an unfair advantage over the mere foot soldiers. Certainly Cooke had taken a big step in first giving Carling such long-term endorsement and then bringing him into the inner sanctum. There was bound to be occasional friction, particularly when you remember that these players spent most of the season in fierce

Brian Moore and Wade Dooley celebrate the try by their captain that would put them into the semi-finals of the World Cup. Brian Moore later described that quarter-final against France as the most brutal match he had ever played in.

MAIN PICTURE: Will Carling shows relief as the final whistle blows in Paris.
TOP INSET: Wade Dooley and Paul Ackford congratulate each other.
BOTTOM INSET: A journey well made. English fans express their joy.

opposition to each other for their clubs. Carling handled the extra responsibility well. He realized very early on, after his first drinking spree with the squad, that he could no longer be one of the lads. Thereafter he kept his distance which suited his nature but helped fuel the myth of aloofness.

Richards sensed his imminent demotion. He vented his own frustration during one of the fiercest training sessions most England players can remember three days before the quarter-final. It was just what the England players needed. It certainly set the scene for what turned out to be a combustible afternoon. Carling has proved himself to be at his best in these times, when England's backs are to the wall and fortitude is called for. His own quiet resolve, that sense of order and stability which surrounds him, was invariably projected to the squad. He has never been a big man for table-thumping or obscenity-laced speeches. He has his gimmicks, from handing out press cuttings of the Murrayfield '90 defeat

prior to the Scotland game the following year to personal letters occasionally sent to the squad, but by and large he played it straight.

There was no need to fire up his men to face the French. They knew it was make or break, and they could sense the red-hot atmosphere outside. Brian Moore vividly described the occasion in his autobiography.

> It was the most ferocious, harsh, brutal match I have played in. It was a constant assault on the senses, occasionally on the body. It was also the most memorable match I have ever played in. As long as I live I will never forget the feeling. It was dangerous and heady, fast-moving and relentless. I felt completely beyond the fear of physical harm. It was the reason I play the game. It was the ultimate feeling of being alive.

Rob Andrew launches the dropped goal that put England into the final of the 1991 Rugby World Cup, after a nerve-racking semi-final against Scotland.

The Andrew up-and-under, the Blanco punch on Heslop, the Skinner tackle on Cecillon, Guscott's break for Underwood's try, France's revival, Carling's late clincher and then, shamefully, the disgraceful assault on referee David Bishop by French coach Daniel Dubroca – all human life was there. England had shown that they had the nerve to be world champions. Now they had to show they had the game to go with it. It was back to Murrayfield.

The demons of that Grand Slam defeat still floated around the stadium. England had enough possession to win the semi-final comfortably. Instead they were almost hung out to dry when Gavin Hastings had a late kick from in front of the posts to make it 9–6. Rob Andrew's drop goal took England through. England had been tight, controlled, minimalist and, to a neutral, incredibly boring. England didn't care. They were in the final.

However much they may have shrugged off the criticism, it was affecting them if only at a subconscious level. They certainly needed to address how close they had come to losing the semi-final. Even though Scotland never really threatened their try line, they had almost sneaked through to steal the match. England had wasted their potential to score and that was the real indictment. They had proven match winners in Guscott and Underwood but they were not being brought into the game.

How would they play it in the final? Everyone predicted that against Australia, England would keep to their strengths. The pack would set the tempo and dictate the pattern of the match. The same crew, more or less, had done it for the Lions. The final would be a re-run of that victorious series. England confounded everyone, including several in their own camp, by playing the game wide. Had they been stung by the media comments? Had

the taunts of that great showman, David Campese, got under their skin? Carling always claimed not. He maintained that the forwards would never have been able to exert the level of control they had achieved against France and Scotland. He figured also that if they kicked and were marginally off-line then Campese and Lynagh would return the ball with interest. So Carling instructed the half backs to open it up. The strategy was not to everyone's taste.

'We should have kicked the leather off it,' wrote Paul Ackford in the *Observer* the following day. Roger Uttley, who retired at the end of the tournament, was equally confused, if not angered.

'I couldn't believe what we were doing,' said Uttley. 'We played into their hands. We had enough of the ball and the game to have seen them off. The World Cup was there for the taking.'

Who was to blame for all this? Some of the senior pros said the decision was a collective one, hatched during the build-up. Once again Will Carling must step into the dock and mount a defence. He still contends there was mileage in the game plan. There was no guarantee of course that England would have won if they had stuck it up the jumper, but the flow of the match suggested they might have done. Carling was not publicly rebuked; in fact the opposite was almost the case. He and the team were fêted as gallant losers, the boys who had run the Aussies so close. Only a try by Daly, and an outrageous deliberate knock-on by the villainous David Campese, had denied them. Inside the camp though there was frustration, particularly among Ackford, Moore, Winterbottom and Teague. They knew they'd had an outstanding chance and they'd blown it.

The one fault which is continually laid at Carling's door is that he is a poor tactician – Cardiff 1989, Murrayfield 1990 and now the World Cup final. He was not solely responsible for the shift in emphasis against

OVERLEAF
MAIN PICTURE: The final whistle blows and England's World Cup dreams are left in tatters.
NSET: Will Carling feels the disappointment at a post-match press conference.

Australia, but if the captain takes the plaudits maybe it's legitimate that he should take the flak as well. There's no doubt that he is not in the same class as either the All Blacks' Buck Shelford or Australian Nick Farr-Jones when it comes to reading a game. There is a naivety about him, evident in this match, and a seeming unwillingness, perhaps an inability, to react on the hoof. He seems to enjoy implementing orders rather than originating them, or at least as far as the nuances of tactical play are concerned. It seemed for this match that England were almost content merely to be there. Of course they fought like dogs to bring the game back to them, to hit the Aussies hard and often and to chase the game until that final whistle blew, but their play lacked that critical edge, induced so often by either fear or overwhelming confidence. In Paris, England had it. The All Blacks

Rory Underwood outpaces Scotland's Craig Chalmers to score England's first try in a 25–7 Five Nations victory. At last the ghosts of 1990 seemed to have been exorcized.

always have it. At Twickenham England did not.

These were blemishes against Carling's name which he struggled to shake off. You might argue that in such an interdependent team sport it's unfair to single out one individual. However, if you aspire to be the best, you have to be judged against the most unforgiving criteria. What Carling could never be accused of is poor sportsmanship. He was dignified and generous in defeat. The same could not be said, in victory, of David Campese.

'If you want to play fifteen-man rugby you have to learn it. You can't just turn up on the day and play that type of game. Australia are used to it; England are not,' was one of the less barbed of Campo's post-final remarks.

There weren't too many tormented England souls sulking in darkened cupboards. The vast majority felt that they had performed creditably, as did the country at large, who fêted the players like never before. However, those players who did feel cheated about the World Cup nursed their feelings in private so that by the time the Five

ABOVE: Trouble flares up at a scrum in yet another ill-tempered match in Paris.
LEFT: Gregoire Lascubé gets his marching orders from referee Stephen Hilditch.

Nations championship swung into view, the simmering sense of unfulfilled potential came bursting out. The World Cup squad was more or less still intact. Only Paul Ackford had retired among the players; on the coaching front, Roger Uttley had been replaced by Dick Best. Will Carling was awarded the OBE in the New Year's Honours List. Geoff Cooke's name was conspicuous by its absence. The Cardiff fiasco had cost him his gong.

Those who found fault with England's approach during the 1991 championship and for much of the World Cup had absolutely no grounds for complaint in the early months of 1992. No side had won back-to-back Grand Slams for almost seventy years. England managed it at a canter, scoring a championship record number of points, 118, in the process. The previous best had been 102 points. They scored fifteen tries in all. It was invigorating stuff. What brought it about? Perhaps some of the ageing England players – Underwood, Skinner, Dooley and Winterbottom – sensed that they would soon join

heavily involved in the hands-on coaching and strategic development of the side. It would be more accurate to see the pair as a partnership than as a hierarchy. It was a successful alliance. England went from being hopelessly unpredictable – fair one match, foul the next – to being ruthlessly efficient. There were lapses, as we have seen, but that tough inner core was keenly honed and apparent for all to see. The secret of a good coach is invariably to get selection right and on that front few could quibble with many of the England sides put out. In particular, Cooke brought together a pack of formidable proportions.

The most subtle question to ponder about the Cooke–Uttley years is whether or not they relied too heavily on their forwards, became too cautious and conservative, particularly when the heat was on. There were certainly many periods when the eye yearned to see more movement, not for its own sake but simply because there was talent out there – Guscott, Carling, Underwood, Halliday – champing at the bit. It's an easy accusation to lob at the two men and a relatively straightforward case to prove. Yes, England were dreadfully cramped and blinkered in the aftermath of Murrayfield 1990. Yes, they did blow a magnificent chance in the World Cup when they tried to turn on the gas too late. But it's convenient to forget just how woefully unproductive England had been prior to the Cooke era, just how starved they had been of that oxygen of success which sustains self-belief. If they went into a shell, there was good reason for it.

We also tend to gloss over those great passages of play which illuminated the run-up to Murrayfield 1990 and the 1992 Grand Slam. If England had not lost that game in Scotland, it's a decent bet that they would have sailed through the early years of the decade playing sumptuous rugby. Of course you cannot ignore the evidence of those years, which saw England riddled with nerves and fear that the expected success would elude them. Looking back from the mid-nineties it has become fashionable to deride England for not developing the fuller, more rounded and expansive game earlier. That is a difficult criticism to justify. England had been on the right road; they were knocked into a siding by Scotland and lost their

way. But winning at any cost was a legitimate target in those days. Only when you have the bedrock of confidence can you strike out more adventurously.

A relative failing which can be pinpointed is that both Cooke and Carling were more conservative and pragmatic than romantic and innovative. Now was the time to move the English game on, to move towards the World Cup of 1995 with new ideas and new personnel. Cooke has been charged with being too loyal to his old guard and not nurturing enough young talent. Again the complaint is a harsh one. Dooley, Winterbottom, Teague, Webb, Underwood and Probyn were all nearing the end of their playing days (or so we thought), and yet they were still proven performers. It was not so much that Cooke was being loyal for loyalty's sake; more that there were so few genuine young contenders hammering at the door. There is a chicken-and-egg situation hovering here. Maybe Cooke might have taken the plunge earlier, given the young ones their head and so encouraged the latent talent. Certainly the southern hemisphere countries have always been far better at trusting in youth. There again, would you prematurely break up a team which had just won a Grand Slam, scoring a record number of points?

If there was an appropriate time for wholesale change, this was it. The start of the 1992–93 season saw a massive alteration in the laws of the game. The International Board dispensed with one of the fundamental tenets of rugby union in decreeing that the ball would be turned over to the other team if it was clogged up in either ruck or maul. For so long the central premise of attack had been that if you were going forward you retained possession. That was no longer necessarily to be the case. At a stroke the pressure platform was dismantled. The new law did not meet with much approval.

'It's a nightmare,' said Australian coach Bob Dwyer. 'The whole thing is madness,' said New Zealand coach Alex Wyllie. 'Do they want us to play rugby league?' inquired Dick Best.

OPPOSITE PAGE: Wade Dooley towers above the rest as England cruise to a comfortable win over Canada. South Africa would provide a sterner test one month later.

MAIN PICTURE: No way through for Canada's Gareth Rees as he is held in his tracks by Will Carling and Dean Ryan with Dean Richards in close attendance during the clash at Wembley.
INSET: Ian Hunter leaps over the line to score his first international try on his England début.

The law was a reality, however, and England, along with the other northern hemisphere countries, were slow to adapt. The championship was to yield only twenty tries, the lowest return for many a year. (England had scored fifteen by themselves in the 1992 tournament.) First, though, there was the now customary autumn double-header to clear. The two-match pre-Christmas routine had sneaked into the schedule almost without notice. It was always Cooke's contention that England needed as much exposure as possible, particularly to southern hemisphere countries. Even in the moments of England's greatest triumphs, when inflated expectation threatened to sway even sensible observers, Cooke was urging caution.

'Until we consistently beat the southern hemisphere countries we will have proved nothing,' he said time and again.

To that end he was keen to get one of the big three on England's early winter schedule. South Africa, back in the sporting fold, were due in November. To prepare for that tough test, Cooke fixed for Canada to come over for a one-off international. Twickenham was undergoing a major overhaul and so England booked in at Wembley. England also played Leicester at the start of the season in a celebration match. There was one familiar name missing from the England team for those early meetings – Rory Underwood. The celebrated winger had announced his retirement at the end of the 1992 season. By the time England faced South Africa on 14 November, Rory had changed his mind. He was back in rugby and back in the side.

England had three new caps in the side which faced Canada: Tony Underwood, Ian Hunter and Victor Ubogu. England won 26–13, Hunter marking his début with two tries.

South Africa were feeling their way back into the rugby world. They had spent a month in France before

New boy Ben Clarke shows the power, pace and athleticism that would make him an integral cog in the England team for years to come.

The Underwood family celebrate Tony's first international try, against South Africa.

Dewi Morris tries to charge down a drop-goal attempt from the legendary South African fly half Naas Botha.

coming to England for the first time in twenty-three years. The French leg had exposed their deficiencies. They lost four of their nine matches there and by the time they arrived in England they were already feeling the strain of being on foreign territory for the first time in many years. England suited them better. They won their matches against the Midlands, the North and England B. They even threatened to upset England, leading 16–11 at half-time. England's greater technical know-how, as well as their fitness, saw them home surprisingly comfortably in the end, 33–16. England introduced another player in that match, Bath No. 8 Ben Clarke. There were to be many rousing battles for the England shirt between him and Dean Richards over the coming months and years. Will Carling scored the final try by following up a steepling Andrew kick. It was a neat way to round off a calendar year, with England undefeated in six matches and Carling himself in the driving seat for the British Lions captaincy.

Of course, if sport obeyed precise formulae no one would watch it. Most of us go to work every day knowing more or less what to expect. We go to watch sport wanting to be thrilled, uplifted and, above all else, surprised. Yes, we want our team to dominate everyone else and to take the title year after year, but we know in our heart of hearts that it will never be like that. Sport has to be erratic and unpredictable, to provide upsets and disappointments, or it is essentially meaningless. Will Carling was set for another tumble.

England were fancied for another unprecedented Grand Slam. They appeared to have the team to succeed: Martin Bayfield was beginning to grow in stature, Ben Clarke to emerge as a vibrant, athletic talent; all the old hands were still on board, through merit rather than misplaced loyalty. But something was missing. As so many sporting sides have found out, staying at the top is often more difficult than getting there. It is not just that other teams are desperate to topple you from your perch: it's also the pressure exerted from within. You've been there before, you've scaled the mountain, the novelty of striving for the unknown is no longer an ever-present stimulant. So much hard work went into the initial achievement, it's almost as if the mind rather than the body switches off at the thought of so much toil and pain again. There is the pressure of expectation and the deadly fear of failure. The constant re-whetting of the appetite is the biggest battle a sportsman ever has to face. Will Carling was struggling within himself to understand these feelings. In his authorized biography, Carling is quoted as saying:

> It dawned on me suddenly this year: why was I playing? Was I captaining England for the right reasons? Was it just ego? I began to question my motives. Was I interested in me, or the team, or in being heralded? Did I want to be the greatest captain there ever was?

Peter Winterbottom and débutant Martin Johnson look on as Dewi Morris releases the England backs during their 16–15 win over France.

ABOVE: Brian Moore makes his point to referee Jim
Fleming during England's clash with France.
LEFT: Ieuan Evans celebrates his match-winning try
against England at Cardiff Arms Park.
OPPOSITE PAGE: Jeff Probyn is held up just short of
the line by the desperate Welsh defence.

Carling thought he had found the answer when the side
slumped in the second match of the championship at that
old burial ground in Cardiff. He found an empathy with
his distressed team-mates. Carling, though, was not back
on track, not at total peace with himself; nor was the team.

Brian Moore was just one of the regular gang who was
going through a difficult patch. If Carling was the
detached, controlled face of England's successful new
order, Moore was its snarling embodiment. For so long,
too long, English sides had seemed afraid to show their

happened to him. He was out of sorts and he knew it. For a while it seemed as if he might go off in a sulk. He was down, homesick, lovesick (he had become engaged to Julia Smith just before the tour started) and wanted to be anywhere else but the back end of New Zealand in mid-winter. There were several others in the party feeling the same. The dirt-trackers (those not in the Test team), reacted badly. Several of them took refuge in booze. Their form and commitment were abysmal. Carling, even though he was low and on the point of quitting the tour, fought back. He has taken part in matches of far greater intensity and of far greater significance, but his play in the match against Waikato, the final midweek game, did him more good than nearly any other in his career. While several others threw in the towel, Carling fought tooth and nail for the Lions' credibility. Once again he had hauled himself up by the bootstraps. His attitude in New Zealand counted for a lot. Even though on paper he had had a woeful summer, he could face the new season and the return of the All Blacks in good heart.

'I'm glad I went through the crisis,' said Carling at the start of the new campaign. 'At one point I very nearly came home. I can't say I enjoyed it all the time but I think it's done me some good. I was scared of being dropped. Once it happened it made me re-evaluate myself. In a perverse way it cleared my mind and restored my enthusiasm. I just wasn't preparing myself or concentrating properly.'

England needed to lick themselves into shape pretty smartly before the All Blacks hit the northern shores at the end of October. The myth of invincibility may have been carrying a slight dent, but no more than that. They would be a formidable trial. By the time they reached Twickenham at the end of November they had won all ten matches and left behind a trail of havoc in Scotland.

England were slowly reconstructing themselves. Dooley, Winterbottom, Teague and Webb had all retired; Jeremy Guscott was on the long-term injury list. During the season Richards, Rodber and Clarke were to join him. It was time for new faces and for those in the background

The England pack provides the perfect platform for Kyran Bracken against the might of the All Blacks.

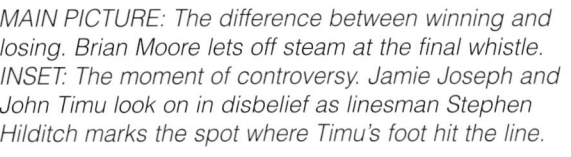

MAIN PICTURE: The difference between winning and losing. Brian Moore lets off steam at the final whistle. INSET: The moment of controversy. Jamie Joseph and John Timu look on in disbelief as linesman Stephen Hilditch marks the spot where Timu's foot hit the line.

to step forward and make their mark. One new face was thrust forward more quickly than anticipated, and it was an All Black who made a mark for all the wrong reasons. Bristol scrum half Kyran Bracken was called up for his début at 48 hours' notice. He got a rousing reception from the crowd and a hostile one from Jamie Joseph. The All Black flanker stamped on the ankle of the prostrate Bracken as the ball moved away from a breakdown. It was a cowardly act, unnoticed by the crowd but picked up by TV cameras and networked that evening on national news bulletins. Bracken hobbled through the game to magnificent effect. His own courage was typical of the team on the day. They stood toe-to-toe with the All Blacks, resisted every charge. The back row of Richards, Clarke and Rodber was awesome. England won 15–9, with four penalties from Callard and a dropped goal from Andrew. Victory completed a clean sweep for Carling against the seven other senior members of the International Board.

There was loose talk every season around this time of year. England must be fancied for a Grand Slam. They've got the forwards to take control and the backs to finish it off. They had to travel to Paris, it's true, but that had caused them no problems in the recent past. All the other countries barely got past passport control before they went weak at the knees at the thought of entering the Parc des Princes. The prospect had the opposite effect on England. They had won there three times in succession, displaying classic English virtues: unflappability, control and pragmatism.

The management team of Dick Best and Geoff Cooke knew that they would have to move the English game on from its dependable base. The question was, how? If the formula of a sturdy pack and dependable fly half was a proven one in the northern hemisphere, why risk changing it? Yet England in their heart of hearts knew they had to develop a more all-round game, a more integrated style of play. It was a search which was to

haunt them for the next three years. Dick Best had all the necessary attributes as well as the right inclinations, but that year he came to realize just how overwhelming the need for victory at this level was, even to the point of sacrificing long-held, cherished notions of playing attacking football. The priority was not to lose. How did he feel about the dawning of this uncomfortable truth?

'I was devastated,' said Best.

Of course Best could have stuck boldly to his principles and encouraged adventure rather than caution, speculated rather than played the percentage game. He was hidebound by the system of domestic league rugby, which was stuck in a rut. Teams were bent on chiselling out victories at any cost. In part, too, Best was finding that English teams had still not come to terms with the new laws. They saw them as something to be endured rather than embraced. The laws were intrinsically daft, it has to be said, yet at the other end of the world the All Blacks were rolling up their sleeves and working on how best to exploit them.

England did actually aspire to moving forward but whenever there was pressure, they reverted to the norm. Carling himself was looking towards new horizons, if only to massage motivation.

'I want us to be more varied in attack,' said Carling as he prepared to face Scotland in the championship opener. 'I personally want to be more involved and help England score more tries. The most important thing for England is to build for the long-term and get things right for 1995. Along the way it would be lovely to win more games than we lose but we have to be brave enough and strong enough to believe that the World Cup is our ultimate goal. You cannot expect perfection all the way for eighteen months. We don't see ourselves as favourites for this game at Murrayfield. We won't be waltzing up there expecting to put on a pretty show.'

In the same breath Carling had revealed the nub of England's dilemma. They wanted to make their game more elaborate yet knew that the game in Edinburgh would be a dog-fight. There was too much pride and national expectation to satisfy to indulge in laboratory experiments. Carling, who led England for the thirty-seventh time, overhauling Nick Farr-Jones's world record, also declared his own agenda.

'I'd love to carry on as captain to the World Cup next year,' he said. 'I can't see myself going on past that. There is a finite period in which you can retain the freshness. As for the record, someone will beat it. It's flattering but it won't make any difference to the England boys. They still fall asleep in team talks.'

England coach Dick Best was aware that true attacking rugby had to be compromised in the search for victory at all costs in the Five Nations Championship.

Gregor Townsend goes for a dropped goal, but Scottish hearts were to be broken by a last-minute, 40-metre penalty by England's Jon Callard.

It was Scotland who were to endure the nightmares after this game. Jon Callard's 40-metre match-winning penalty goal in the last minute silenced the crowd and reduced Gavin Hastings to tears. Hastings was rebuked by some snide, small-minded commentators for his public show of emotion. If anything Hastings's tears confirmed the difficulties which confronted Best and England. The Five Nations is a such a fraught, passionate affair, one which means so much to players and spectators alike, that it is a monumental task to consider using it as a means to some hypothetical end. It is an end in itself and victory is all-important.

England had their victory in the bag and were on their way towards what many observers deemed the key game

– Le Crunch (Part IV) in Paris in a month's time. The only obstacle in the way was the Irish at Twickenham. Ireland had only won once at Twickenham in eighteen years and had been thumped in Paris on the opening day of the championship. Will Carling had never tasted defeat at home in six years as captain. Cue the upset. Ireland not only won, 13–12, they won in style, scoring the game's only try, a splendidly worked effort from Geoghegan. Most disturbingly for England, this was the fourth match in succession in which they had failed to score a try.

This lack of an attacking edge had plagued England on and off for a few years. They explained away 1991 as a mental hangover from the Grand Slam loss at

Simon Geoghegan rounds Tony Underwood to score his try in Ireland's 13–12 victory. It was only the second win for Ireland at Twickenham in eighteen years.

LEFT: Philippe Sella, Rory Underwood and Tim Rodber decide on a game of catch.
RIGHT: England's man mountain, Dean Richards, controls matters in the pack.

riposte from England. Gallic flair pitted against Anglo-Saxon sangfroid. It had made for one hell of a confrontation in recent times and so it proved again. England had made five changes from the Irish match – Pears, Hunter, Morris, Redman and Ojomoh for Callard, Tony Underwood, Bracken, Bayfield and Back. England went down the usual route, Rob Andrew's boot (five penalties and a dropped goal) seeing them home 18–14. This was their fourth win in a row in Paris and their seventh in succession against France.

There was one other significant change made in the week leading up to the game – that of the manager, Geoff Cooke. To the surprise of everyone, Cooke announced that he would retire at the end of the championship. The players were stunned and the rugby world was stunned. Had he jumped or had he been pushed? There was talk of knives in the back, some RFU men finally getting their revenge for the Cardiff fiasco. It was a neat and dramatically satisfying theory, but Cooke dismissed it out of hand. He'd had enough, pure and simple.

'I've grown weary of living in the goldfish bowl,' he said.

He didn't categorically refute the charge that he had not always got on with some sections of the hierarchy – he'd further alienated the blazers for his defence of Wade Dooley's predicament on the Lions tour – but he insisted that his decision was personal and straightforward. He was no longer enjoying the experience and so, with the demands on his time increasing, he thought it only fair to finish in time for someone else to get their feet under the table before the World Cup.

Who would that be? There was only one serious runner – Jack Rowell of Bath. The RFU for once reacted with haste and good sense and Rowell was duly appointed. Several questions clamoured for attention. Now that Cooke was on his way, how long before Carling followed in the same direction, not necessarily of his own volition? The same was true of Dick Best. The final conundrum was more immediate. Would England send

Murrayfield. They broke free the following year to run up their highest ever points total in the championship. For the last two years, though, they had been inconsistent; usually resolute and disciplined but rarely sparkling. One of the complaints levelled later, by colleagues such as Jeremy Guscott, was that the midfield axis of Andrew and Carling was too similar and too predictable. The taunt will go with them to the grave, for there can be no denying the record books which show that England did not rattle up points as often or as emphatically as they might have done.

What Andrew and Carling did offer England was once again on show in Paris. Another cauldron; another cool

MAIN PICTURE: Ieuan Evans raises the Five Nations Championship trophy.
INSET TOP LEFT: Brian Moore shows his feelings as England fail to secure the championship. Despite defeating Wales, they came second on points difference.
INSET TOP RIGHT: Jack Rowell – England's man for the future.
INSET BOTTOM RIGHT: Geoff Cooke, who announced his retirement at the end of the 1994 Five Nations.

off Cooke with a flourish against Wales? The Grand Slam and Triple Crown were up for grabs for Wales; the title for England or Wales. Even though they showed far more wit and invention, England could not make up the 16-point differential. They won the match 15–8, but Wales took the trophy.

Who knows what might have befallen England if Cooke had stayed on the bridge directing operations. His track record – two Grand Slams and a World Cup final – is only part of the story. He reinvented English rugby, gave it an identity and a purpose. He instilled a sense of belief and ruthlessness in his players, gave the structure of the game a much-needed dust-down and focus. The question of whether England would have succeeded anyway without Will Carling's contribution has been answered in part already; essentially Carling was but a part of the whole. There will be no argument in stating that Cooke's influence was overpowering and almost wholly beneficial. His contribution was knocked retrospectively as England struggled in their bid to play total rugby in the 1995 World Cup. In the revisionist process, Cooke was indicted for his deep-rooted conservatism. That judgement is too one eyed and unforgiving. There were times, it's true, when England settled for a guaranteed return rather than gambling for glory. The failing was one of nerve, not ability. Cooke's teams had shown in early 1990 and throughout 1992 that they could play with dash and style and still be effective. Cooke built the foundations; he was the architect of success where none had existed before. It was up to others to carry it on.

The South African tour in May 1994 proved a formative experience. The Test series itself was drawn, with England scoring an unlikely but magnificent triumph in the first Test in Pretoria, 32–15, before bowing to the Springbok backlash a week later in Cape Town, 27–9. It was not these matches which so radically

MAIN PICTURE: Ben Clarke dives over the line to score during England's 32–15 victory over South Africa in Pretoria.
INSET LEFT: Celebration time.
IINSET RIGHT: Rob Andrew's try rounded off a superb afternoon. He collected 27 points in the match.

infiltrated English thinking. Rather it was the spirit of rugby abroad in the country, at provincial, under-21 and youth level, which made such an impression on the party. In the build-up to the first Test, as England travelled to the Orange Free State, Natal, Western Transvaal and Transvaal, they experienced the same brand of dynamic, expressive rugby which was to become the hallmark of the All Blacks a year later. England, meanwhile, carried on kicking their lines and kicking for goal, waiting for others to make mistakes.

'It's a crying shame,' admitted Les Cusworth one evening. 'We've got to move on.'

England's final tour record of three wins from eight matches was stark testimony to their deficiencies. Tim Rodber became the first Englishman for nineteen years to be sent off when he was dismissed against Eastern Province. Bristol's Paul Hull won his first cap at full back. These were the minor details of a major tour. England would be back in South Africa within the year. The World Cup was looming, and England were off the pace.

MAIN PICTURE: François Pienaar keeps South Africa in control. England came down to earth with a bang in the second Test played at Cape Town as they crashed 27–9. INSET: Will Carling feels the strain during the second Test defeat. They now knew what to expect in the World Cup in a year's time.

Chapter Seven

1994–95:
High hopes and hot air

Rugby was a multi-million pound industry. Matches at Twickenham, which grossed £1.5 million, were four times over-subscribed for tickets; sponsors were falling over themselves to be associated with the game; and the World Cup, which was to round off this season, was on line to make profits running to many millions of pounds.

For all the wealth and supposedly professional infrastructure, the old game could still behave with extraordinary cack-handedness and insensitivity. Two events illustrate the point. At the beginning of the season, Dick Best was sacked; at the end Will Carling was. Of course, in streamlined commercial circles people are sacked every day and there is nothing untoward or ethically wrong in this. However, there were different circumstances here. The Carling old farts affair was obviously far more of a major news event than Best's dismissal. The RFU itself was far more culpable in the stance it adopted, but it should also shoulder blame for the manner in which Best was ditched.

Best's days appeared to be numbered from the moment Jack Rowell took over from Geoff Cooke. Rowell had always been his own man at Bath. He is an imposing figure with strong views and a desire to be totally involved. Even though he had been appointed manager there was little doubt that he would want a large say in the routine running of the show. Best felt that at the time and was surprised when he was not asked to move aside before the South African tour. Rowell had brought in Les Cusworth, but only as assistant coach. Best was still the main man, shaping the style and tactics of the team. Rowell took a very backward seat on the tour, rarely interfering and letting Best have his head. The tour was not a success overall, although Best's side had pulled off that stunning win in the first Test in Pretoria.

Best returned home and was busy preparing individual videos for each player for the forthcoming season when there was a knock at his door late one evening. It was a close friend, Graham Smith, who had worked alongside Best as manager of London and who was now on the RFU's national playing committee. He also happened to be godfather to Best's daughter. He'd taken it upon himself to tip off Best that he was to get the axe the next day. If he hadn't done so, Best might well have learnt the news from the press. It was a tawdry handling of the situation.

There is no denying that Jack Rowell had every right to run the show in his own way. Even Best accepted the logic of that on the grounds that too many cooks can quickly spoil the broth. The RFU had the perfect opportunity to bring all that about without loss of face to anyone soon after Geoff Cooke resigned. Instead Best, whose record as England coach (won thirteen from seventeen matches, including one Grand Slam and victories over New Zealand and South Africa) stands comparison with the best of them, was dumped in ignominious fashion.

Jack Rowell had clear ideas about the way in which he wanted England to evolve in the run-up to the World Cup. In many ways they differed very little on paper from Best's own outlook when he had first come on to the international scene. But, as Best had discovered, there is a world of difference between club and international level in terms of opposition, public pressure and players' attitudes. Rowell, however, is a strong man who relished the opportunity all the more for it being difficult.

'We need a more dynamic, complex game,' said Rowell. 'The modern international scene demands it. Forwards have to react in a more positive fashion and there has to be more integration between forwards and backs. This is the reality of the modern game. It is nothing to do with providing what is called entertainment and everything to do with giving players more chances to score tries. A try is worth more points than a penalty and

so if you score a lot of them you have a better chance of winning. It's as simple as that.'

Rowell could point to the reference books for anyone who doubted the validity of what he was saying. In the 1993–94 season England had stuttered. In four of their five matches they had failed to score a try. As Rowell said: 'What's the point of having Rory Underwood in your side if you don't use him?'

That, then, was the game plan. How to get this across to the players? It would be easy enough to read the last few paragraphs to them, see them nod their heads in agreement and then trot out on to the training pitch and sit back as they put it into practice. It's never as easy as that, or we could all be great managers. Rowell knew that he had to get the players to discover the truth for themselves. They had to believe that it was the best way forward, so that when the pressure came on in the middle of a match they would not revert to type and start kicking the length of the field again.

One of the key men in making all this happen would be the fly half. Barnes or Andrew? It might have been a fascinating twist to the old story, but Barnes had gone. He announced his retirement on returning from South Africa

It was a surprise decision, particularly to Rowell. He and Barnes went back a long way at Bath. Barnes appeared to be Rowell's type of man: strong-minded, maverick, feisty, intelligent, brave, headstrong and imaginative.

'Stuart Barnes is a one-off,' Rowell once said. 'He has an on-board computer which runs through all the available options in an instant. He's the equivalent of the American quarter back and it needs a very special man to be that.'

Yet when it came to the crunch Rowell had opted for Rob Andrew. On the South African trip Andrew was in pole position. Barnes was struggling a bit with injury, it's true, but he was still fit enough to play for the midweek side against South Africa A at Kimberley, a game which was lost but which many saw as the turning point prior to the first Test. Barnes was never given the Saturday slot. Of course, Dick Best was a major voice on selection; Rowell had deliberately adopted a back-seat position. So Andrew got the nod.

Who knows what Rowell might have done? He's never been an easy man to predict. He certainly has a way of keeping people on their toes. Where Cooke was methodical and straightforward, Rowell is spiky and enigmatic. A lot of this is almost gamesmanship. He arrived with a reputation for being a hard, no-nonsense type, used to getting his own way, be it in business or at Bath. He would stir people up, weed out the weak, lay in to the lazy, kick-start the back line into action, make English rugby seek out and reach new horizons. The list went on and on. Part of it was truthful assessment; part just fanciful myth. Rowell had no intention of playing down the contrived parts. Why should he if it had the desired effect?

'Perhaps everything was a bit cosy,' said Rob Andrew. 'We all need a change of stimulus from time to time, and I certainly felt challenged when Jack came in.'

Andrew responded positively to the situation, which is no more than we would expect of the man. If Brian Moore has to bare his teeth and strip menacing black tape across his forehead to express his commitment, Rob

Tony Underwood scythes his way through the Romanian defence during England's comprehensive 54–3 victory.

Andrew does it in a less overt, less theatrical but no less emphatic manner. He never shirks a tackle, is meticulous in his preparation, is as involved and competitive at whatever level he performs, and guards his shirt with the tenacity and zeal of a Samurai warrior. You just don't see it so brazenly, that's all. There is no ego shrieking for attention in Rob Andrew. He gets on with it in his unobtrusive, unfussy way. When he realized that he was in line to be England's front-line kicker for the season he reacted in typical fashion. He fixed up coaching sessions with kicking expert Dave Alred. At the end of a hard-working week, and after a tough Saturday game somewhere, Rob Andrew would take himself off down the M4 from London on a Sunday morning for a couple of hours tuition from Alred in Bristol.

All the toil and endeavour paid off. England's two pre-Christmas internationals were against Romania and Canada. In the first match, which England won, 54–3, Andrew banged over ten goals from eleven place kicks. A month later he had corrected that slight flaw and returned a perfect score – twelve goals from twelve attempts, on a blustery day to boot, and equalled the

Practice makes perfect. Rob Andrew with another successful goal on his way to a new world record points tally – later broken in the World Cup by Gavin Hastings and then New Zealand's Simon Culhane.

Kyran Bracken rounds the last line of defence to score his first international try in England's match with Canada.

world record for most points (thirty) in a major international. It was not just Andrew in the groove. England hit superb form to beat Canada 60–19. Rowell's words seemed to have struck a chord.

The players themselves were eager both for success and for acclaim. The players may all say that they take no notice of the press, but they do. It's not so much that the comments made by the media are necessarily right. It's more that every sportsman wants to be loved as well as to be successful. It's the tone of comment rather than its precise point of reference which carries weight. Of course the far greater spur was their own desire to excel, to nurture their collective game so as to be in a position to face and meet the challenge of the rest of the world nine months later in South Africa.

Will Carling may have been personally disappointed to see Dick Best go, a man he regarded as something of a confidant, but he was determined to move forward in the best interests of England. He echoed many of the thoughts of Rob Andrew.

'I accept that there might have been a bit of a comfort zone,' said Carling. 'We have to improve our game for the future. Jack has said that he would like me to lead us to the World Cup provided I am playing well enough to hold my place in the team. I wouldn't want it any other way. I thought perhaps I was beginning to play too much to a certain style, to take tackles and be a foil for Jerry. I want to create space and cause a lot of problems for the opposing defence.'

He was to do that all right, as well as to create a few problems for the RFU. However, on the rugby front, things were moving smoothly. The players took it upon themselves to fix monthly gatherings at Marlow during the early winter, an enormous commitment for those with full-time jobs and a distance to travel. But the end of the rainbow beckoned in South Africa and the hard work was endured willingly.

There was a sense throughout the season that England were in this together. In part this evolved through natural means. They spent so much time in each other's company

through Marlow training night and the build-up to the internationals as well as the World Cup itself, that some degree of bonding was inevitable. In part, however, the situation was manufactured by Rowell. He wanted to involve the players in the decision-making process, make them aware of the broad picture as well as of their own specific and particular tasks. There was no attempt to downgrade Carling's own role; merely to re-define and possibly enhance it. Carling thrived on it.

'You can only go so far with a team by telling them,' he said. 'To win the World Cup we shall need leaders throughout the side. That's not captaincy by committee but co-ordination.'

The warm-up matches against Romania and Canada offered tantalizing evidence that the squad were beginning to gel and that Rowell's long-term goal was being realized many months ahead of schedule. There were twelve tries scored in the two matches, a couple of them in the Canadian match by substitute Mike Catt. Catt came on for Paul Hull, who had been one of the successes of the summer tour to South Africa. Catt made the most of his opportunity. Even though not a full back either by inclination or by experience, he kept the No. 15 shirt right through the season. Poor Hull, who was fit by the New Year, could only watch from the sidelines in frustration. He did not even have the consolation of a World Cup place, with Ian Hunter and Jon Callard being taken as cover full backs.

While Hull was suffering, England were prospering. They knew better than anyone that the Romanians and Canadians were phoney battles. The Romanians had lost to Oxford University the week before the Test while Canada were to lose all six matches of their tour of Italy, England and France. They still had to be subdued, of course, and the points scored. The real test was the Five Nations. Could England's vaunted ambitions stand the strain of the championship, with all its passion, rivalry and history?

No one could doubt the statistical record. England saw off all comers for the third time in five years. Will Carling became the first captain to lead a country to three Grand Slams. England had poise, method, bright intention and

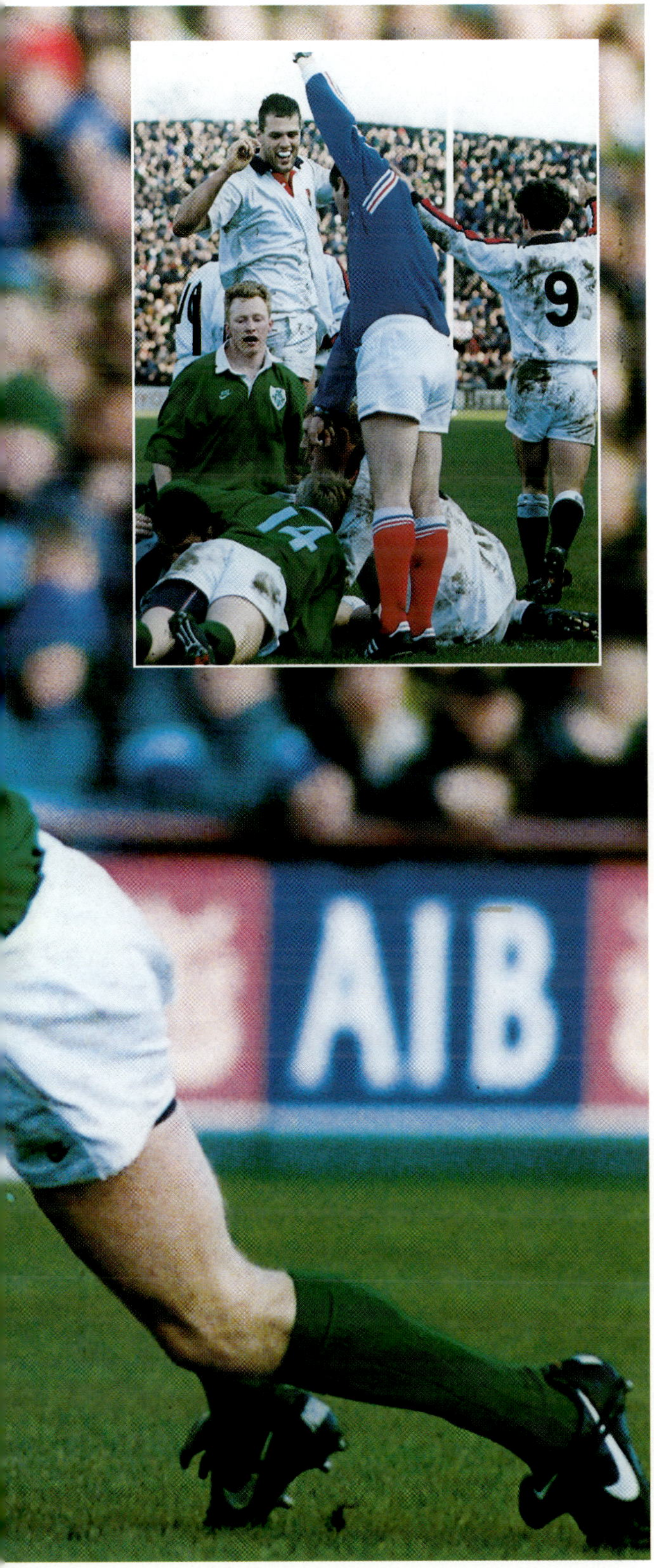

MAIN PICTURE: *Will Carling, supported by Ben Clarke, takes on the Irish defence.*
INSET: *Ben Clarke dives over the line to score in England's 20–8 win in Dublin.*

bursts of clinical and even spectacular efficiency. They scored 98 points in all, unearthed a strike-running full back in Mike Catt, lorded it over France for the eighth time in succession and, all in all, appeared to be in decent shape for the World Cup.

The tone of the season was set within the first ten minutes of a fascinating match in Dublin which opened the championship. The goalposts were rocking in the howling wind, the crowd were at their throatiest and England knew that the Irish team would be whipping up their usual stormy reception committee. England quelled the tempest in green with stern forward control and hard-running strike play. (They could do nothing about the winds which blew all day.) Only six minutes had run on the clock before Carling corkscrewed his way over the line. Ben Clarke followed a quarter of an hour later with Tony Underwood rounding off a good day at the office for the men in white shirts with a second-half try.

England have had the measure of France so often that we ought not to have been surprised when France, who again promised so much coming into the match at Twickenham, seemed to freeze when confronted by the perfidious Anglo-Saxons. England never looked like losing as Tony Underwood scored a brace of tries, Guscott the other. England won 31–10, the biggest victory over France since the First World War.

The trip to Cardiff is no longer a journey into mental purgatory. If you need a benchmark of how far England had come in the Carling years, this observation is perhaps it. There are no more terrors, real or imagined, to confront. Wales, who gave England a tough test for the forwards, went down 23–9, the tries this time coming from the other half of the Underwood family, Rory, who scored two, and Victor Ubogu.

Nine tries in all and a Grand Slam to tilt for. Surprisingly, there was another team going for it as well – Scotland. There was so much recent history to contend with, so many rich tribal attachments either to endorse or reject, that it was no surprise when the match was hyped

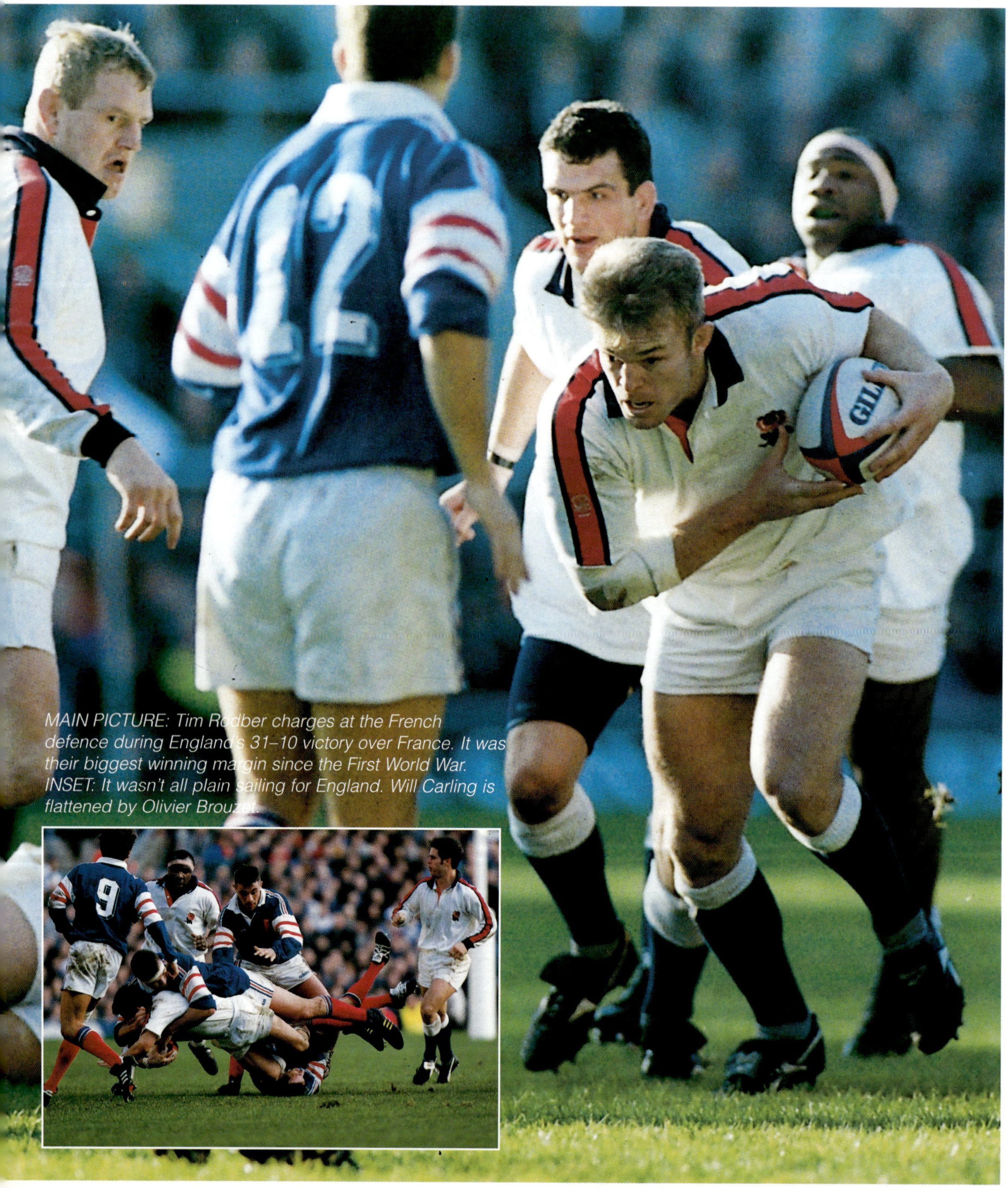

MAIN PICTURE: Tim Rodber charges at the French defence during England's 31–10 victory over France. It was their biggest winning margin since the First World War.
INSET: It wasn't all plain sailing for England. Will Carling is flattened by Olivier Brouzet.

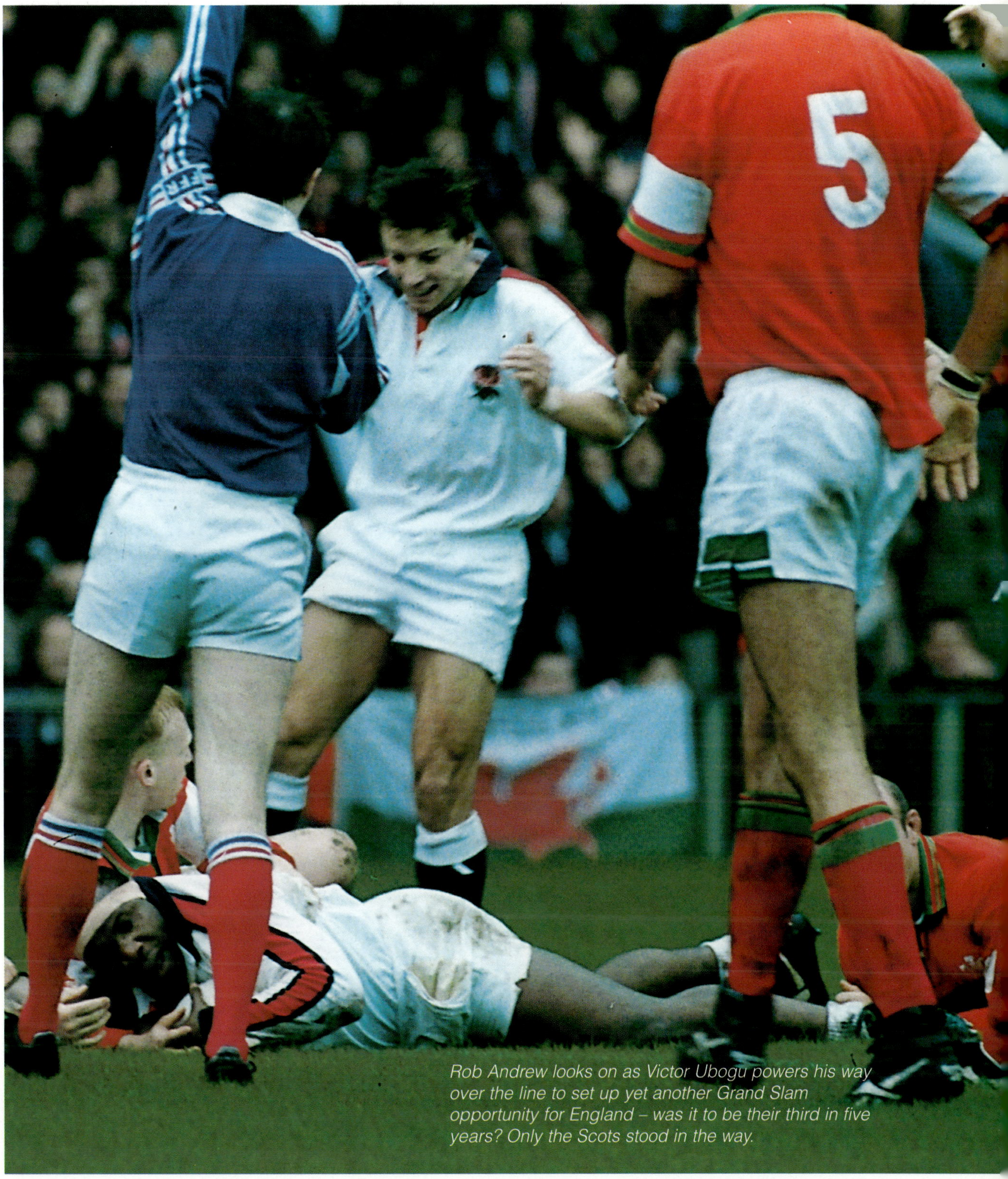

Rob Andrew looks on as Victor Ubogu powers his way over the line to set up yet another Grand Slam opportunity for England – was it to be their third in five years? Only the Scots stood in the way.

MAIN PICTURE: A now-familiar scene as Will Carling's England secure their third Grand Slam in five years – even if the manner of victory did not quite live up to the pre-match billing. Rob Andrew (INSET) chipped in with all of England's points (seven penalties and a dropped goal). As Dick Best had previously discovered, winning is everything in the Five Nations.

out of all proportion. Tickets were changing hands at £1,500 a pair and what did we get – anti-climax. England won 24–12, Andrew bagging seven penalties and a dropped goal. Andrew finished with 24 points in all to equal the championship record set by Sebastien Viars of France in 1992. Jason Leonard became England's most-capped prop. England managed to get through the championship unchanged, only the sixth side ever to do so.

So England had records, trophies and stability. They appeared to be on perfect course. You had to look closely to detect a flaw, but it was there all right. Brian Moore rebuked Scotland on television immediately afterwards for killing the game and ruining the match as a spectacle. Moore was right to a degree. The significant point he glossed over was that England had failed to stop the Scots doing this, had failed to impose their own style and their own rhythm. Opponents are supposed to be a pain, to be obstructive and irritating. If England couldn't get to grips with Scotland, how would they fare with the big boys from the southern hemisphere? It wasn't just the Scots who were meddling with England's World Cup prospects. The gods above were also intent on mixing in a little mayhem.

The build-up was almost complete. All that remained was the Pilkington Cup final between Bath and Wasps. England had eight of the World Cup party on parade and if they could just get through that unscathed. . .

The cup final was to be the least of Jack Rowell's problems that weekend. On Thursday night Channel 4 broadcast a programme called 'Fair Game', part of a series which looked at current issues in different sports. In it, Will Carling was heard to say: 'If the game is run properly as a professional game, you do not need fifty-seven old farts running rugby.'

It was a throwaway line, delivered off-camera. Most of the rugby world saw it as a joke comment. It was not the funniest nor the most original line ever delivered and smacked very much of public schoolboy humour. It's the sort of remark overheard a hundred times in clubhouses every weekend. In fact, it's tame by comparison with some of the things said. The RFU did not see it that way.

Six of them – Dennis Easby, Ian Beer, Bill Bishop, John Richardson, Peter Bromage and John Motum – convened on Friday evening either in person or by telephone. By that time Carling had issued an apology. It was too late. Next morning, the day of the cup final itself, Carling was sacked. England were a fortnight away from the World Cup. They were near the end of four years of preparation and they had dismissed the sport's most successful ever captain. It was perhaps the most monumental cock-up in the history of English rugby.

Carling is no saint and had been hauled over the coals a couple of times in his career before. He is not to everyone's liking. Some find him too self-driven, too much of a loner to be truly hugged to the bosom as a great bloke. Others see his steadfastness and commitment to the England cause as a mark of greatness. Whatever else was proved over that weekend, it was clear that the public loved him.

The outcry against the sacking was enormous, far greater than any of us imagined it would be. The RFU were rocked on their heels. Throughout Sunday the phone lines hummed as everyone contemplated the screaming headlines and prime-time TV news bulletins. Carling's agent, Jon Holmes, took it upon himself to call Easby and propose a meeting. Easby agreed and by Monday morning the white flag of surrender was being run up over Twickenham. It wasn't quite presented as capitulation, of course, but that's how the public saw it.

'I regret what I said,' said Carling. 'I should not have said it. I would like to thank Dennis [Easby] because I put him in a situation I regret.'

Easby, too, played a diplomatic bat.

'Will and I had a very good meeting. He gave me all the assurances I needed. Will's original apology was not quite sufficient.'

Jack Rowell commented: 'Will put his foot in it. But the situation has been restored through the grace of the president. It has been the most interesting Bank Holiday ever for me but we hope that we are stronger for this ordeal.'

In that Rowell was right. The England players, galvanized by Dean Richards and Rob Andrew, had

MAIN PICTURE: Jack Rowell looks on in disbelief as England fail to recapture any form during their opening group matches.
INSET TOP: Rory Underwood surges through a gap in the Italian defence to score the first of England's tries.
INSET BOTTOM: The Argentinian pack power their way over the line.

Neil Back crosses the line to score for England in a much-improved performance against Western Samoa. Despite a number of changes to the side, England could go into their quarter-final clash with renewed confidence.

rallied squarely behind Carling. They would need every last drop of that solidarity over the next five weeks in South Africa.

The World Cup had been at the centre of England's thoughts for the previous four years. That is not to say that they were able to tailor every last second of preparation to that end. There were too many outside distractions to achieve that, too many unforeseen circumstances to make the passage from one tournament to another a smooth one. England's entire management structure had changed; several players – Dooley, Winterbottom, Teague among them – had retired. Will Carling was one of the constants; so too were Brian Moore, Rob Andrew and Jerry Guscott, safely rehabilitated during the season after a worrying twelve-month lay-off with a pelvic injury. They had kept the World Cup in their sights all that time. Now it was here.

England were based in Durban for their matches. They had wanted to be out of town in a secluded five-star resort complex. The World Cup organizers insisted that all the teams should have the same standard of accommodation. The days ticked by as England geared up for the opening. They trained hard under blue skies and endless sun. Their three pool matches were against Argentina, Italy and Western Samoa. On paper for England it was a perfect group. England should win all three matches but would be tested in different areas in every one. The Argentinians were powerful scrummagers, perhaps the best in the tournament; the Italians were less robust but meddlesome nonetheless, while the Samoans had flair, strong runners and fearsome tacklers. England won through but rarely strung together much in the way of fluency or dominance.

Argentina were eventually beaten 24–18, even though they scored two tries to England's six penalties and two dropped goals. Italy proved a handful. Andrew again was on form with the boot, scoring seventeen points in all to see England home 27–20. It had not been an auspicious start, and certainly not one to worry the southern hemisphere, particularly the men in black who unleashed the boy wonder Jonah Lomu on the world.

England hit the higher notes against Western Samoa,

however. There was more width to their game, more conviction and pattern to their running. England won 44–22, Rory Underwood grabbing a couple of tries, Neil Back the other. There was also a penalty try. England were through to the quarter-finals, where they would play Australia. Time for a spot of revenge?

The picture of Rob Andrew's last-second drop-goal winner flashed round the world. It was a dramatic end to a gripping match. England displayed all their traditional virtues – resolve, commitment, organization with an occasional splash of flair. Tony Underwood scored a sparkling try after twenty minutes, outstripping the defence in a 55-metre run as England swooped on an Australian mistake. Damian Smith scored a try in the first minute of the second half for Australia. Lynagh and Andrew traded kicks and the match was deadlocked at 22–22. A final line-out, Bayfield taps, Andrew swings the boot from 45 metres and an entire nation goes potty.

Their delirium was put into perspective a week later. Same day, Sunday; same stadium, Newlands, Cape Town; totally different result and performance. Jonah Lomu ran all over England with a black tide of his mates in support. England's World Cup was over, smashed 45–29 by New Zealand. (There was still the third place play-off to go against France, which was lost 19–9, but it was a sideshow.)

There was only one question to ponder: how good were New Zealand; how poor were England? The team itself grasped at consolation straws, claiming that they had hit back superbly in the second half and even put together some of that elusive dynamic rugby. They were deluding themselves. The All Blacks were way ahead by the time England started to play. They had switched off the mental burners for sure and were gliding towards the final. They led 35–3 after fifty-one minutes. They were entitled to coast.

England were not beaten by Jonah Lomu alone, although, admittedly, he was rather a large slab of icing on the cake. New Zealand showed that they had greater pace and dynamic power, surer skills under pressure, better integrated teamwork and a much deeper-rooted intention to play an all-round game. It was the game

The image which shot around the world. Rob Andrew's last-minute dropped-goal put England into the semi-final but England were to be brought down to earth the following weekend.

Rob Andrew consoles the England captain as all World Cup dreams were blown apart by a staggering All Black performance in the first fifteen minutes of the contest.

England aspired to. South Africa may have shut the All Blacks out in the final by playing a classic northern-hemisphere type of game, but the sport was moving in a different direction.

The future lay elsewhere. England had to go in that direction. It was a journey which was to cause Carling and Rowell yet more angst over the next twelve months.

Will Carling, though, had a little domestic problem to sort out first.

Although Jonah Lomu cut an immense and destructive figure during the World Cup semi-final, many thought that he alone was not the difference between the two sides. England still had a long way to go.

Chapter Eight

1995–96: The final curtain

Will Carling thought he had it bad back in 1991. One of the causes of the Cardiff post-match silence had been the excessive demands of the media. The players felt put upon, occasionally hounded and they wanted to make a stand. It was all nonsense, of course. Carling himself quickly realized that.

Four years later he had cause to look back on those days as a time of innocence. News of his alleged affair with Princess Diana broke during August. There was scarcely a moment that Will Carling could truly call his own for the next nine months. He may have achieved a certain fame as England's rugby captain. It was as nothing to the notoriety he earned as a friend of the most famous woman in the world. As a result of the story, Carling could not step outside the door of his house in Putney without a hundred camera lenses zooming in on him. His phone number was changed constantly to keep him one step ahead of the royal rat-pack. He even had to check his wastepaper bin carefully lest he should inadvertently throw away something from which they might draw their own conclusions. When you move in Royal circles, your dustbins are no longer your own.

Two things happened as a result of all this. Carling's marriage broke up and he played some of the best rugby of his life. There is no doubt that these were traumatic times for Will Carling. They would have been if he had been a workaday centre threequarter for Putney Third XV. Marriage is a rather major part of one's life and when it disintegrates it takes its toll. Quite who was to blame in all this is irrelevant as far as these pages are concerned. What does concern us is the impact it had on Carling's rugby. At club level in particular, it flourished. He had been slated just twelve months earlier in the *Daily Telegraph* by a former England colleague, Stuart Barnes, for what Barnes saw as a desperate lack of commitment on Carling's part when he was wearing the colours of the

Harlequins. Carling himself had admitted enough times down the years that his prime interest and priority was country, not club. But now, perhaps for the first time in his life, he was treating his club rugby not as a means to an end but in exactly the same way as thousands of players up and down the land – as an escape from domestic strife.

The club were good to him. They protected him from undue hassle from the media, they gave him a shoulder to cry on and they provided a focus during those distracting times. There was another little cloud floating across the Carling landscape. It was announced at the end of August that Carling would carry on as England captain. At least it was announced by Carling. The RFU itself had not actually approved the matter and so we had yet another farcical month during which everyone denied that anything had been agreed, yet stated that there was nothing sinister in Carling not being appointed just yet.

'When I became manager last year I believed in him,' said Rowell. 'His leadership has improved since I have been manager. It's not an issue. I am relaxed about it and I expect Will is too.'

Will said he was relaxed about it but no one really believed him. This was a public snub. In a perverse way perhaps it was fortunate that he had so many other things on his mind, because he might well have dwelt more on the relationship between himself and Jack Rowell. It was never an easy, harmonious one.

There is nothing too surprising about this. Many players, of different temperaments and backgrounds, bury their latent antipathy for the greater good of the English cause. Brian Moore and Graham Dawe barely exchanged a word during the eight years of their intense rivalry. Finally, in South Africa, they happened to be at the bar together, struck up a conversation and each found that the other one wasn't such a bad bloke after all. According to common myth, Geoff Cooke and Will

Carling were bosom buddies. They weren't at all. They were on the same wavelength in many matters but they didn't live in each other's pockets.

There was no reason to suspect that Rowell and Carling would be soulmates. In fact it was a good bet when Rowell was appointed that Carling would not last the course. Rowell wanted to change England's ways and attitudes, to move on from what he perceived to be the

just underway, several of the old guard were nearing the end of their playing careers and Rowell wanted to build for the future. Maybe in another era Carling might have stepped down voluntarily. But the season had another minor little change to take on board – that of professionalism.

The announcement in Paris that the sport was to go fully pro plunged the game, in Britain in particular, into

François Pienaar leads the South African charge at Twickenham, on the way to his side's comprehensive 24–14 victory.

narrow confines of Geoff Cooke's style. Carling was the epitome of that earnest but too often shackled approach. But Rowell did put his faith in Carling and was duly rewarded.

But what now? It would have been the perfect opportunity for a change. The new World Cup cycle was

turmoil. No one quite knew what to expect. (They still don't, but that's another story.) Suddenly there were new challenges, exciting developments and unexpected horizons. Carling, along with many players, was stimulated by the prospect. This had little to do with the fact that their pockets were to be lined and everything to do with finally being able to contemplate devoting themselves full-time to their sport. It was no time to consider stepping aside.

'At last we're an honest game,' said Carling. 'Rugby's credibility has taken a hammering with the constant denial of what, in many places, has been an obvious truth – that players were being paid to play rugby. I was staggered, absolutely staggered, by the IB's decision. But I'm all for it. To some it may all sound horrendous but it won't be if we manage the change. And it will all be for the greater good. A strong England at international level

all year about his true feelings. The pair, throughout what was to be a roller-coaster campaign, trotted out the usual diplomatic platitudes. There was, they said, no tension or friction between them. Privately, several insiders told a different story. There were so many periods during the season when England appeared confused, lacking focus and harmony both on and off the pitch. By the season's end they had won the championship again so we ought

is good for the domestic as well as the world game.'

How good would England be? How much had they learnt from the World Cup? It took some time to find out. Jack Rowell did eventually confirm Carling as captain. The offer did not come until relatively late. The first training squad for the South African match in November was named as early as late September. Carling's name was there all right, but without the usual accompanying brackets. Rowell was to keep his cards close to his chest

Chester Williams crosses the line once again as South Africa show their overall superiority over England. The Springbok winger was denied a hat-trick only by a controversial refereeing decision.

perhaps to accept the management line that this was a season of development and experiment, that the troubles were no more than the natural growing pains of any side.

Several new faces were introduced during the season. The championship half backs were from second-division

England's new half-back partnership, Northampton's Matthew Dawson and Paul Grayson (INSET) were drafted in to face Western Samoa.

Northampton, Matt Dawson and Paul Grayson; Lawrence Dallaglio of Wasps became a fixture on the England openside, Leicester's Graham Rowntree the resident loose head with Bristol's Mark Regan for company alongside. Garath Archer, who did a quick flit from Newcastle to Bristol and back again, steamed into the second row midway through the year. Dewi Morris had retired, Brian Moore came back out of retirement, then went back into it again, and Rob Andrew accepted a hefty chunk of Sir John Hall's millions and headed north to Newcastle.

Rowell himself was bent on injecting his squad with fresh ideas. As ever, the admirable theory had practical complications. As he approached the first match of the season, against the world champions, no less, Rowell was in a quandary. His two fly halves, Mike Catt and David Pears, were battling against injury; two of his props, Jason Leonard and Victor Ubogu, were short of fitness.

'This is no way to get in shape to meet the world champions,' said Rowell a few days before the match. 'We're still looking to expand, but not too fast. You can become too loose and too predictable. Perhaps that's why the All Blacks lost the World Cup final. I'm looking for integrated rugby, with forwards driving upfield so that everyone plays with the ball in hand.'

He could but dream. England played poorly against South Africa. The final margin was only ten points, the Boks winning 24–14, but in nearly every phase England were out-thought and out-fought. South Africa scored three tries, had another perfectly good one disallowed and England only got over the line on the stroke of full-time when de Glanville, who had come on for the injured Carling, crossed. It was back to the drawing board.

For the Western Samoa match a month later Rowell made several changes. Out went the specialist openside flanker, Andy Robinson, whom Rowell had recalled to the colours after a six-year absence. Mike Catt, who had been paraded by Rowell as the man to fill Rob Andrew's boots for a long time to come, found himself shunted

back to the full-back position. None of it was much use. England struggled once again. They won 27–9 in the end but both their tries had a mundane point of origin in the scrum. It was Western Samoa who played the livelier, more inventive and dynamic rugby. The crowd, who jeered England at one point, were confused; so too were the players. Before the match Rowell had said:

'The stop–start game has been rapidly outmoded since the World Cup and either we get into it or we will be left behind. England owes the nation a big one. They owe themselves a big one.'

After the match Rowell said:

'The players were too wound up with trying to play the so-called champagne rugby. . . we tried to handle the ball in the wrong places and I blame the media for that . . . I'd rather we got back to basics and where we were in last year's Five Nations.'

That was no bad place to be, given that England had scored nine tries in their first three games. But Rowell was sending out all the wrong signals. He fell out with many in the media, accusing them of stirring things up and criticizing unfairly. The players themselves were unsure about how to proceed. Rowell and Carling were not communicating effectively with each other, so perhaps it was no surprise that the right messages were not getting through to the players. Rowell was intent on shifting the means of communication itself. He did not believe in precise instruction for the simple reason that matches very rarely obey precise criteria. The players had to learn to think for themselves.

It was a painful experience. Having basked in a warm glow from the moment of his succession right through to the start of the World Cup, Rowell was now beginning to feel the heat. He may even have at last begun to appreciate the pressures and strains endured by his predecessors, Dick Best and Geoff Cooke. They too, at various stages, had had grand designs on playing a more rounded game. Best, in particular, had been hit hard by the crippling realization that victory was the be all and end all at international level.

Rowell himself tried to play down expectations, appealing to the public to have patience, to accept a few

losses along the way which would be a small price to pay if long-term success came about. He was whistling in the wind. No one was listening. This was the Five Nations. This was England's territory. Supporters would not stand for second best.

England travelled to Paris for the opening match. What greater test could there be of a side's backbone than a quick dip into the Parc des Princes cauldron. In fact, such a tough opener suited England perfectly. As

They drove deep, the ball was recycled, Castaignède swung a hopeful boot and the ball went through the posts – 15–12 to France, but England had reclaimed some of the lost ground.

What had they learnt? That the team had a solid base, could withstand pressure, and had a decent kicker in Paul Grayson. There was one note of real hope – the form of débutant winger Jon Sleightholme of Bath. He had been unheralded but his hustling defence, eager eye for the

The form of Bath's Jon Sleightholme was one of the many encouraging signs for Jack Rowell and the England management team following the defeat in Paris.
LEFT: Thomas Castaignède celebrates his last-minute match-winning drop goal.

underdogs they had nothing to lose. France had broken that long run of England success at the World Cup and they also had an All Black scalp under their belts from the first Test in Toulouse a few months earlier. England were up against it. How did they respond? In the usual way, with guts, purpose, resolution and spirit. They seemed to have done enough when Paul Grayson banged over an equalizing penalty goal with just a couple of minutes left, but France had one last plunge for glory left in them.

break and speed off the mark proved to be considerable assets during the course of the season.

No sooner had England poked their head out of the tunnel than they were back inside it, consumed by

darkness, a fortnight later. They beat Wales 21–15 but it was a hesitant, hidebound England on show. It was Wales who made much of the running. They lost through their own errors and immaturity. They had put their faith in youth, an investment repaid handsomely when fly half Arwel Thomas tapped a penalty kick to himself and caught England napping as he set up the position from which Hemi Taylor scored. England ground out their win. Rory Underwood got a try back for England to put them ahead 7–5 at the break. Then came Wales's moment of madness, a charged-down kick letting in Guscott for a try. Grayson, who had a woeful afternoon, did manage to

Mike Catt congratulates Rory Underwood on his try against Wales.
LEFT: Hemi Taylor dives over the line to give Wales the lead at Twickenham. The advantage was short-lived as England went on to win the game 21–15.

knock over three penalties to give England the cushion to withstand Wales's late charge. Victory to England but the storm clouds were beginning to break.

There had been mutterings in the press of dissension in the camp in the build-up to the match. Everyone played it down but, in the immediate aftermath of this game, Rowell was overheard by a TV reporter saying: 'I don't

MAIN PICTURE: The England pack hold a committee meeting chaired by Dean Richards who, on his return, had a magnificent game for England to deny the Scots a Grand Slam.
INSET: New cap Garath Archer, who was thrown in at the deep end, into the Murrayfield cauldron.

believe what I am seeing.' Later he was more public, in declaring:

'The game plan we aspire to is not mine. It is ours. A lot of the sessions are run by the captain and the players. As far as I am concerned we are in it together.'

Rowell was under pressure. It got worse. England had a month to prepare to meet Scotland. They announced the team early. Martin Bayfield and Tim Rodber were dropped. In came two players from the opposite ends of the international spectrum: new boy Garath Archer and old sweat Dean Richards. Former England second row Paul Ackford was apoplectic about the selections. In a column in the *Daily Telegraph* he railed against the confusion of Rowell's regime.

'The latest England selection has descended into farce. Jack Rowell has completely lost the plot.'

There was a certain logic behind Ackford's ire. Rodber had been dropped for the first match then recalled against Wales without playing a club game in between. He had played reasonably well against Wales, only to find himself dropped again. Bayfield, too, had cause to feel aggrieved. England had changed hookers. Mark Regan had his moments but had still not hit a perfect throwing groove.

The spotlight swung round on to Rowell. Ackford's comments made a stir. Up until then, Rowell had more or less kept his counsel, but he decided to go on the offensive in defence of his policies.

'I am very confident that we are going in the right direction,' he said. 'I have to accept the pressure but I ask that people put the whole thing in perspective. The criticisms are mind-boggling.'

Rowell had a modicum of right and reason on his side but he failed to own up to the limitations and deficiencies of the team. A few days later at Murrayfield little of it mattered to the general public as England throttled a Scottish Grand Slam. The man who did it was the man Rowell had brought back – Dean Richards.

Deano controlled the ball and with it the tempo of the match. The Scots sent the ball his way right from the kick-off. They barely saw it again. England won 18–9 (all penalties, wouldn't you know) and returned home in upbeat mood. They left behind some disgruntled Scots.

'I feel so sorry for the people who paid to watch such a disgraceful exhibition of rugby,' said former Scottish full back Andy Irvine.

What was it Brian Moore had said a year before about the Scots killing the game? The scoresheet from the last three encounters between these two countries made for depressing reading: they had scored just one try between them in 240 minutes of rugby.

Where did all this leave England? Here are a couple of lines from Will Carling.

'Sometimes people don't understand the passion that goes into Five Nations rugby,' he said. 'Sometimes it's a bit too easy to say "play free-flowing rugby".'

Sound familiar? You could pick any one of the eight years of Carling's reign and the remark would not be out of place. It's not that he's necessarily wrong; more that nothing much seems to have changed in the English psyche during that time. There has been phenomenal success, and that must never be understated or undervalued. The Grand Slams were great achievements for English rugby and for Will Carling. Where Carling is wrong is to cite the exigencies of the Five Nations as an excuse, as if the pressure of those matches was any greater than that of a World Cup semi-final, or that the rivalry was that exceptional. Neither point is true. The All Blacks stuck to their expansive game against England and reaped a wonderful reward. They ran set-piece ball from the very first minute, attacked from their own 22, and England were crushed. Of course the emotion underpinning the Five Nations is real and enduring, but is it really any more intense than the rivalry which exists between Aussies and Kiwis? I doubt it. Yet these two teams have given us some of the great matches of the last decade.

Perhaps Will Carling realized all this and decided it was time for someone else to have a go. It was time to step down. Carling announced his decision the week before the last match of the season, against Ireland at Twickenham. The news was broken in his *Mail on Sunday* newspaper column. Maybe Carling owed the

RIGHT: *Will Carling leads England out as captain for the last time, against Ireland.*

RFU no favours; maybe he wasn't too bothered about Jack Rowell's reaction, either. The public had little idea where the news appeared first. The protocol might be a minor irritant but there were some who felt that the announcement should have been made formally.

There was no quibbling with Carling's overall contribution, however. Whatever the troughs, whatever the blips and blots, the rows with the RFU, he ended hugely in credit. He led England fifty-nine times and notched up forty-four wins. No other captain in the history of the game gets anyway near his aggregate record. He was an icon of his time, ambitious, progressive, hard-edged and a careerist. That latter description is no criticism. The public took time to warm to him, for he was not a Bill Beaumont, cauliflower-eared type, but warm to him they did. When he took over there were very few schoolboys who would bother to decorate their walls with posters of England rugby players. By the time he stepped down he was as well-known and popular as Mike Atherton or David Platt; more so, in fact. There may have been friction on a very few occasions with the media, but there was never any hint of impatience with young supporters. Carling has always done an enormous amount of work with kids, a lot of which goes unpublicized.

Carling's timing was perfect. It gave him the moral high ground to quit while he was ahead. He had survived two seasons with Jack Rowell. There was a strong sense that he would not make a third.

'It is time the captaincy moved on,' said Carling. 'I thought after the World Cup that I could provide some continuity while the inevitable rebuilding took place. After eight years I'm going to miss it terribly. It's hard to give up something which has changed my life, 99 per cent of it for the better.'

There was praise from nearly every quarter. Roger Uttley was one of the few to inject a touch of reality and common sense into all the hyperbole when he pointed out that Carling had benefited from having so many strong individuals around him during those early years.

A twisted ankle provided a somewhat anti-climactic end to Will Carling's career as England captain.

Significantly, Carling himself was one of the first to point this out in his retirement comments.

'You are only as good as the decision-makers around,' he said. 'I owe a huge amount to those guys. I can still have a quiet beer with the likes of Mike Teague, Peter Winterbottom and Wade Dooley knowing that there is a deep, lasting friendship.'

Carling had given England something which one hopes will last. No longer are England under-achievers; no longer is Twickenham viewed as any old stadium where the result can go either way. Carling helped make Twickenham a venue to be proud of and, if you were an opponent, to be feared. For the stability he represented and for the pride and dignity he helped restore to the English rose, it's to be hoped that the legacy is not wasted.

The final image of Will Carling is of him hobbling up the steps at the end of the match against Ireland to collect the Millennium Trophy, awarded to the winners of that particular game. Carling had come off with an injured ankle after barely half an hour's play, but England had gone on to win 28–15 and with it the championship, France having lost in Cardiff. It was a final twist to an extraordinary tale. Carling carries on, of course, as a mere player. He has even threatened to switch to fly half. We have not heard the last of him.

Will Carling views the last moments of the 1996 Five Nations Championship from the stands. There was some consolation, though, as Wales's surprise victory over France in Cardiff gave England the title.

Results: 1988–96

1988-89

5 November 1988, Twickenham

England 28
Tries Underwood (2), Morris, Halliday
Conversions Webb (3)
Penalty Goals Webb (2)

Australia 19
Tries Leeds, Campese, Grant
Conversions Lynagh (2)
Penalty Goal Lynagh

England:

JM Webb	PAG Rendall
	BC Moore
AT Harriman	JA Probyn
WDC Carling (c)	
SJ Halliday	WA Dooley
R Underwood	PJ Ackford
	DW Egerton
CR Andrew	D Richards
CD Morris	RA Robinson

Replacement:
JDR Buckton (for Carling)

Australia:

AJ Leeds	MN Hartill
	TA Lawton
JC Grant	AJ McIntyre
B Girvan	
MT Cook	SAG Cutler
DI Campese	WA Campbell
	JS Miller
MP Lynagh	SN Tuynman
NC Farr-Jones (c)	JM Gardner

Referee: DJ Bishop (New Zealand)

---

4 February 1989, Twickenham

England 12

Penalty Goals Andrew (2), Webb (2)

Scotland 12
Try Jeffrey
Conversion Dods
Penalty Goals Dods (2)

England:

JM Webb	PAG Rendall
	BC Moore
R Underwood	JA Probyn
WDC Carling (c)	
SJ Halliday	WA Dooley
C Oti	PJ Ackford
	MC Teague
CR Andrew	D Richards
CD Morris	RA Robinson

Referee: G Maurette (France)

Scotland:

PW Dods	DMB Sole
	KS Milne
KW Robertson	AP Burnell
S Hastings	
SRP Lineen	CA Gray
I Tukalo	DF Cronin
	J Jeffrey
CM Chalmers	DB White
G Armstrong	F Calder (c)

---

18 February 1989, Lansdowne Road

Ireland 3

Penalty Goal Kiernan

England 16
Tries Moore, Richards
Conversion Andrew
Penalty Goals Andrew (2)

Ireland:

FJ Dunlea	TJP Clancy
	SJ Smith
MJ Kiernan	JJ McCoy
BJ Mullin	
DG Irwin	DG Lenihan
KD Crossan	WA Anderson
	PM Matthews (c)
PM Dean	NP Mannion
LFP Aherne	PTJ O'Hara

Replacement:
BJ Spillane (for O'Hara)
Referee: LJ Peard (Wales)

England:

JM Webb	PAG Rendall
	BC Moore
R Underwood	JA Probyn
WDC Carling (c)	
SJ Halliday	WA Dooley
C Oti	PA Ackford
	MC Teague
CR Andrew	D Richards
CD Morris	RA Robinson

Replacement:
GJ Chilcott (for Probyn)

---

4 March 1989, Twickenham

England 11
Tries Carling, Robinson
Penalty Goal Andrew

France 0

England:

JM Webb	PAG Rendall
	BC Moore
R Underwood	JA Probyn
WDC Carling (c)	
SJ Halliday	WA Dooley
C Oti	PJ Ackford
	MC Teague
CR Andrew	D Richards
CD Morris	RA Robinson

France:

S Blanco	P Ondarts
	P Dintrans
J-B Lafond	C Portolan
P Sella	
M Andrieu	G Bourguignon
P Lagisquet	J Condom
	M Cecillon
F Mesnel	L Rodriguez
P Berbizier (c)	D Erbani

Replacements:
J-P Garuet (for Portolan)
D Charvet (for Lagisquet)

Referee: SR Hilditch (Ireland)

---

18 March 1989, Cardiff Arms Park

Wales 12
Try Hall
Conversion Thorburn
Penalty Goals Thorburn (2)

England 9

Penalty Goals Andrew (2)
Dropped Goal Andrew

Wales:

PH Thorburn (c)	M Griffiths
	IJ Watkins
IC Evans	L Delaney
DW Evans	
MR Hall	PT Davies
A Emyr	RL Norster
	G Jones
P Turner	MA Jones
RN Jones	DJ Bryant

England:

JM Webb	PAG Rendall
	BC Moore
R Underwood	GJ Chilcott
WDC Carling (c)	
SJ Halliday	WA Dooley
C Oti	PJ Ackford
	MC Teague
CR Andrew	D Richards
CD Morris	RA Robinson

Replacement:
GW Rees (for Teague)

Referee: KVJ Fitzgerald (Australia)

---

13 May 1989, 23 August Stadium, Bucharest

Romania 3

Penalty Goal Ignat

England 58
Tries Oti (4), Guscott (3), Probyn, Richards
Conversions Hodgkinson (8)
Penalty Goal Hodgkinson
Dropped Goal Andrew

Romania:

M Toader	G Leonte
	V Ion
N Racean	G Dumitrescu
N Fulina	
A Lungu	S Ciorascu
D Boldor	G Caragea
	F Murariu (c)
G Ignat	H Dumitras
D Neaga	A Radulescu

Replacements:
C Raducanu (for Caragea)
T Oroian (for Radulescu)
Referee: JB Anderson (Scotland)

England:

SD Hodgkinson	PAG Rendall
	BC Moore
R Underwood	GJ Chilcott
JC Guscott	
SJ Halliday	PJ Ackford
C Oti	WA Dooley
	MC Teague
CR Andrew (c)	D Richards
SM Bates	PJ Winterbottom

Replacements:
JA Probyn (for Chilcott)
GW Rees (for Richards)

1989-90

4 November 1989, Twickenham
England 58
Tries Underwood (5), Skinner, Bailey, Linnett, Ackford, Guscott
Conversions Hodgkinson (5), Andrew
Penalty Goals Hodgkinson (2)

Fiji 23
Tries Eranavula Teleni, Rasari, Savai
Conversions Koroduadua (2)
Penalty Goal Koroduadua

England:
SD Hodgkinson	MS Linnett
	BC Moore
R Underwood	AR Mullins
JC Guscott	
WDC Carling (c)	WA Dooley
MD Bailey	PJ Ackford
	MG Skinner
CR Andrew	PJ Winterbottom
RJ Hill	DW Egerton

Fiji:
Naituilagilagi	Taga
	Naiviliwasa
Lovo	S Naituku
Eranavula	
Nadruku	Savai
Vonolagi	Rasari
	Matirawa
Koroduadua	Dere
Vasuwulagi	Teleni (c)

Referee: BW Stirling (Ireland)

20 January 1990, Twickenham
England 23
Tries Underwood, Probyn, Carling, Guscott
Conversions Hodgkinson (2)
Penalty Goal Hodgkinson

Ireland 0

England:
SD Hodgkinson	PAG Rendall
	BC Moore
R Underwood	JA Probyn
WDC Carling (c)	
JC Guscott	PJ Ackford
MD Bailey	WA Dooley
	MG Skinner
CR Andrew	DW Egerton
RJ Hill	PJ Winterbottom

Ireland:
K Murphy	DC Fitzgerald
	SJ Smith
MJ Kiernan	G Halpin
BJ Mullin	
DG Irwin	NPJ Francis
KD Crossan	WA Anderson (c)
	PM Matthews
P Russell	NP Mannion
LFP Aherne	PTJ O'Hara
Replacement:	
JP MacDonald (for Smith)	

Referee: P Robin (France)

3 February 1990, Parc des Princes
France 7
Try Lagisquet

Penalty Goal Charvet

England 26
Tries Underwood, Guscott, Carling
Conversion Hodgkinson
Penalty Goals Hodgkinson (4)

France:
S Blanco	P Ondarts
	L Armary
M Andrieu	J-P Garuet
P Sella	
D Charvet	T Devergie
P Lagisquet	D Erbani
	O Roumat
F Mesnel	L Rodriguez (c)
P Berbizier	E Champ
Replacement:	
P Marocco (for Armary)	

England:
SD Hodgkinson	PAG Rendall
	BC Moore
R Underwood	JA Probyn
WDC Carling (c)	
JC Guscott	PJ Ackford
MD Bailey	WA Dooley
	MG Skinner
CR Andrew	MC Teague
RJ Hill	PJ Winterbottom

Referee: OE Doyle (Ireland)

17 February 1990, Twickenham
England 34
Tries Carling, Underwood (2), Hill
Conversions Hodgkinson (3)
Penalty Goals Hodgkinson (4)

Wales 6
Try Davies

Conversion Thorburn

England:
SD Hodgkinson	PAG Rendall
	BC Moore
SJ Halliday	JA Probyn
JC Guscott	
WDC Carling (c)	PJ Ackford
R Underwood	WA Dooley
	MG Skinner
CR Andrew	MC Teague
RJ Hill	PJ Winterbottom

Wales:
PH Thorburn	M Griffiths
	KH Phillips
MH Titley	L Delaney
MG Ring	
MR Hall	GO Llewellyn
A Emyr	AG Allen
	PT Davies
DW Evans	MA Jones
RN Jones (c)	RG Collins

Referee: D Leslie (Scotland)

17 March 1990, Murrayfield
Scotland 13
Try Stanger
Penalty Goals Chalmers (3)

England 7
Try Guscott
Penalty Goal Hodgkinson

Scotland:
AG Hastings	DMB Sole (c)
	KS Milne
AG Stanger	AP Burnell
S Hastings	
SRP Lineen	CA Gray
I Tukalo	DF Cronin
	J Jeffrey
CM Chalmers	DB White
G Armstrong	F Calder
Replacement: DJ Turnbull (for White)	

England:
SD Hodgkinson	PAG Rendall
	BC Moore
SJ Halliday	JA Probyn
JC Guscott	
WDC Carling (c)	PJ Ackford
R Underwood	WA Dooley
	MG Skinner
CR Andrew	MC Teague
RJ Hill	PJ Winterbottom

Referee: DJ Bishop (New Zealand)

1 May 1990, Battaglini Stadium, Rovigo
Italy XV 15
Try Cuttitta
Conversion Troiani
Penalty Goals Troiani (3)

England XV 33
Tries Oti, Buckton, Back, Andrew
Conversions Hodgkinson (4)
Penalty Goals Hodgkinson (2)
Dropped Goal Andrew

Italy XV:
L Troiani	G Grespan
	C Pratichetti
E Venturi	A Piazza
J Morelli	
S Barba	R Saetti
Marcello Cuttitta	R Favaro
	M Pedroni
M Bonomi	C Covi (c)
F Pietrosanti	P Reale
Replacements:	
G Pivetta (for Pratichetti)	
L Francescato (for Pietrosanti)	
D Tebaldi (for Bonomi)	

England XV:
SD Hodgkinson	MS Linnett
	BC Moore
NJ Heslop	JA Probyn
WDC Carling (c)	
JDR Buckton	R Kimmins
C Oti	WA Dooley
	NA Back
CR Andrew	DA Cusani
SM Bates	J Wells
Replacements:	
CJ Olver (for Moore)	
JF Clough (for Carling)	

Referee: P Frantschi (France)

1990-91

28 July 1990, Velez Sarsfield Stadium, Buenos Aires
Argentina 12   **England 25**
Tries Oti, Ryan
Conversion Hodgkinson
Penalty Goals Cosa (4)   *Penalty Goals* Hodgkinson (5)

Argentina:
A Scolni | A Rocca
| J-J Angelillo
H Vidou | L Molina
M Loffreda (c)
D Cuesta Silva | E Branca
S Salvat | A Iachetti
| PA Garreton
R Madero | M Baeck
F Gomez | MJS Bertranou

England:
SD Hodgkinson | J Leonard
| BC Moore
NJ Heslop | JA Probyn
WDC Carling (c)
JDR Buckton | NC Redman
C Oti | WA Dooley
| MG Skinner
D Pears | D Ryan
RJ Hill | PJ Winterbottom

Referee: B Kinsey (Australia)

4 August 1990, Velez Sarsfield Stadium, Buenos Aires
Argentina 15   **England 13**
Tries Hodgkinson, Heslop
Conversion Hodgkinson
Penalty Goals Vidou (5)   *Penalty Goal* Hodgkinson

Argentina:
A Scolni | M Aguirre
| J-J Angelillo
H Vidou | DM Cash
M Loffreda (c)
D Cuesta Silva | E Branca
S Salvat | A Iachetti
| PA Garreton
R Madero | M Baeck
F Gomez | MJS Bertranou

England:
SD Hodgkinson | J Leonard
| BC Moore
NJ Heslop | JA Probyn
WDC Carling (c)
JDR Buckton | NC Redman
C Oti | WA Dooley
| MG Skinner
D Pears | D Ryan
RJ Hill | PJ Winterbottom
Replacement:
DW Egerton (for Dooley)

Referee: B Kinsey (Australia)

29 September 1990, Twickenham
England 18   **Barbarians 16**
Tries Richards, Hodgkinson   *Tries* Campese, Davies
Conversions Hodgkinson (2)   *Conversion* Lynagh
Penalty Goals Hodgkinson (2)   *Penalty Goals* Lynagh (2)

England:
SD Hodgkinson | J Leonard
| CJ Olver
T Underwood | JA Probyn
WDC Carling (c)
JC Guscott | PJ Ackford
R Underwood | WA Dooley
| MC Teague
CR Andrew | D Richards
RJ Hill | PJ Winterbottom
Replacement:
GW Rees (for Winterbottom)

Barbarians:
K Murphy | RW Loe
| IJ Watkins
J-B Lafond | AP Burnell
JT Stanley
D Charvet | ID Jones
DI Campese | SAG Cutler
| K Janik
MP Lynagh | PT Davies
NC Farr-Jones (c) | EJ Rush
Replacement:
NA Back (for Janik)

Referee: WD Bevan (Wales)

3 November 1990, Twickenham
England 51   **Argentina 0**
Tries Underwood (3), Guscott (2),
Hill, Hall
Conversions Hodgkinson (7)
Penalty Goals Hodgkinson (3)

England:
SD Hodgkinson | J Leonard
| CJ Olver
NJ Heslop | JA Probyn
WDC Carling (c)
JC Guscott | PJ Ackford
R Underwood | WA Dooley
| JP Hall
CR Andrew | D Richards
RJ Hill | PJ Winterbottom
Replacement:
GW Rees (for Ackford)

Argentina:
A Scolni | F Mendez
| RA Le Fort
S Ezcurra | DM Cash
D Cuesta Silva
M Allen | G Llanes
GM Jorge | PL Sporleder
| PA Garreton
H Porta (c) | AM Macome
G Camardon | MJS Bertranou

Referee: CJ Hawke (New Zealand)

19 January 1991, Cardiff Arms Park
Wales 6   **England 25**
    Try Teague
Penalty Goals Thorburn, Jenkins   *Penalty Goals* Hodgkinson (7)

Wales:
PH Thorburn (c) | BR Williams
| KH Phillips
IC Evans | P Knight
MG Ring
IS Gibbs | Glyn Llewellyn
SP Ford | Gareth Llewellyn
| AJ Carter
NR Jenkins | P Arnold
RN Jones | GM George
Replacement:
CJ Bridges (for Jones)

England:
SD Hodgkinson | J Leonard
| BC Moore
NJ Heslop | JA Probyn
WDC Carling (c)
JC Guscott | PJ Ackford
R Underwood | WA Dooley
| MC Teague
CR Andrew | D Richards
RJ Hill | PJ Winterbottom

Referee: RJ Megson (Scotland)

16 February 1991, Twickenham
England 21   **Scotland 12**
Try Heslop
Conversion Hodgkinson
Penalty Goals Hodgkinson (5)   *Penalty Goals* Chalmers (4)

England:
SD Hodgkinson | J Leonard
| BC Moore
NJ Heslop | JA Probyn
WDC Carling (c)
JC Guscott | PJ Ackford
R Underwood | WA Dooley
| MC Teague
CR Andrew | D Richards
RJ Hill | PJ Winterbottom

Scotland:
AG Hastings | DMB Sole (c)
| KS Milne
AG Stanger | AP Burnell
SRP Lineen
S Hastings | CA Gray
A Moore | DF Cronin
| DJ Turnbull
CM Chalmers | DB White
G Armstrong | J Jeffrey

Referee: SR Hilditch (Ireland)

2 March 1991, Lansdowne Road

Ireland 7
Try Geoghegan

Penalty Goal BA Smith

England 16
Tries Underwood, Teague
Conversion Hodgkinson
Penalty Goals Hodgkinson (2)

Ireland:

JE Staples	JJ Fitzgerald
	SJ Smith
SP Geoghegan	DC Fitzgerald
BJ Mullin	
DM Curtis	NPJ Francis
KD Crossan	BJ Rigney
	PM Matthews
BA Smith	BF Robinson
R Saunders (c)	GF Hamilton

England:

SD Hodgkinson	J Leonard
	BC Moore
NJ Heslop	JA Probyn
WDC Carling (c)	
JC Guscott	PJ Ackford
R Underwood	WA Dooley
	MC Teague
CR Andrew	D Richards
RJ Hill	PJ Winterbottom

Referee: A Ceccon (France)

16 March 1991, Twickenham

England 21
Try Underwood

Conversion Hodgkinson
Penalty Goals Hodgkinson (4)
Dropped Goal Andrew

France 19
Tries Saint-André, Camberabero, Mesnel
Conversions Camberabero (2)
Penalty Goal Camberabero

England:

SD Hodgkinson	J Leonard
	BC Moore
NJ Heslop	JA Probyn
WDC Carling (c)	
JC Guscott	PJ Ackford
R Underwood	WA Dooley
	MC Teague
CR Andrew	D Richards
RJ Hill	PJ Winterbottom

France:

S Blanco	G Lascubé
	P Marocco
J-B Lafond	P Ondarts
P Sella	
F Mesnel	M Tachdjian
P Saint-André	O Roumat
	X Blond
D Camberabero	A Benazzi
P Berbizier (c)	L Cabannes

Replacement:
M Cecillon (for Tachdjian)

Referee: LJ Peard (Wales)

1991-92

20 July 1991, Suva

Fiji 12
Try Seru
Conversion Serevi
Penalty Goal Serevi
Dropped Goal Serevi

England 28
Tries Probyn, Underwood, Andrew
Conversions Webb (2)
Penalty Goals Webb (2)
Dropped Goals Andrew (2)

Fiji:

O Turuva	M Taga (c)
	S Naivilawasa
F Seru	E Naituivau
J Taqaiwai	
V Rauluni	I Savai
T Vonolagi	S Domoni
	I Tawake
W Serevi	M Olsson
P Tabulutu	A Dere

England:

JM Webb	J Leonard
	BC Moore
R Underwood	JA Probyn
WDC Carling (c)	
JC Guscott	NC Redman
C Oti	MC Bayfield
	MC Teague
CR Andrew	D Richards
RJ Hill	GW Rees

Replacement:
MG Skinner (for Teague)

Referee: B Kinsey (Australia)

27 July 1991, Sydney

Australia 40
Tries Campese (2), Ofahengaue (2), Roebuck
Conversions Lynagh (4)
Penalty Goals Lynagh (4)

England 15
Try Guscott
Conversion Webb
Penalty Goals Webb (3)

Australia:

MC Roebuck	AJ Daly
	PN Kearns
DI Campese	EJA McKenzie
JS Little	
TJ Horan	RJ McCall
RH Egerton	JA Eales
	V Ofahengaue
MP Lynagh	TB Gavin
NC Farr-Jones (c)	SP Poidevin

Replacement:
PJ Slattery (for Farr-Jones)

England:

JM Webb	J Leonard
	BC Moore
R Underwood	JA Probyn
WDC Carling (c)	
JC Guscott	MC Bayfield
C Oti	PJ Ackford
	MC Teague
CR Andrew	D Richards
RJ Hill	PJ Winterbottom

Referee: K Lawrence (New Zealand)

WORLD CUP 1991

POOL I

3 October 1991, Twickenham

England 12

Penalty Goals Webb (3)
Dropped Goal Andrew

New Zealand 18
Try M Jones
Conversion Fox
Penalty Goals Fox (4)

England:

JM Webb	J Leonard
	BC Moore
R Underwood	JA Probyn
WDC Carling (c)	
JC Guscott	PJ Ackford
C Oti	WA Dooley
	MC Teague
CR Andrew	D Richards
RJ Hill	PJ Winterbottom

New Zealand:

TJ Wright	SC McDowell
	SBT Fitzpatrick
JJ Kirwan	RW Loe
CR Innes	
BJ McCahill	ID Jones
JKR Timu	GW Whetton (c)
	AJ Whetton
GJ Fox	MN Jones
GTM Bachop	ZV Brooke

Replacement:
AT Earl (for Brooke)

Referee: JM Fleming (Scotland)

8 October 1991, Twickenham
England 36
Tries Underwood, Guscott (2), Webb
Conversions Webb (4)
Penalty Goals Webb (4)

Italy 6
Try Marcello Cuttitta
Conversion Dominguez

England:
JM Webb	J Leonard
	BC Moore
C Oti	JA Probyn
WDC Carling (c)	
JC Guscott	PJ Ackford
R Underwood	NC Redman
	MC Teague
CR Andrew	D Richards
RJ Hill	PJ Winterbottom

Replacement:
PAG Rendall (for Probyn)
Referee: JB Anderson (Scotland)

Italy:
L Troiani	Massimo Cuttitta
	G Pivetta
P Vaccari	F Properzi Curti
S Barba	
F Gaetaniello	R Favaro
Marcello Cuttitta	G Croci
	R Saetti
D Dominguez	M Giovanelli
I Francescato	G Zanon (c)

Replacement:
M Bonomi (for Trioani)

---

11 October 1991, Twickenham
England 37
Tries Underwood (2), Carling, Skinner, Heslop
Conversions Hodgkinson (4)
Penalty Goals Hodgkinson (3)

USA 9
Try Nelson
Conversion Williams
Penalty Goal Williams

England:
SD Hodgkinson	J Leonard
	CJ Olver
NJ Heslop	GS Pearce
WDC Carling (c)	
SJ Halliday	NC Redman
R Underwood	WA Dooley
	MG Skinner
CR Andrew	D Richards
RJ Hill	GW Rees

Referee: LJ Peard (Wales)

USA:
RB Nelson	L Manga
	AW Flay
GM Hein	N Mottram
MA Williams	
KG Higgins	KR Swords (c)
P Sheehy	CE Tunnacliffe
	S Lipman
CP O'Brien	R Farley
MD Pidcock	AM Ridnell

Replacements:
MG de Jong (for Higgins)
JP Wilkerson (for Farley)

QUARTER-FINAL
19 October 1991, Parc des Princes, Paris
France 10
Try Lafond

Penalty Goals Lacroix (2)

England 19
Tries Underwood, Carling
Conversion Webb
Penalty Goals Webb (3)

France:
S Blanco (c)	P Ondarts
	P Marocco
J-B Lafond	G Lascubé
P Sella	
F Mesnel	O Roumat
P Saint-André	J-M Cadieu
	E Champ
T Lacroix	L Cabannes
F Galthié	M Cecillon

Referee: DJ Bishop (New Zealand)

England:
JM Webb	J Leonard
	BC Moore
NJ Heslop	JA Probyn
WDC Carling(c)	
JC Guscott	PJ Ackford
R Underwood	WA Dooley
	MG Skinner
CR Andrew	MC Teague
RJ Hill	PJ Winterbottom

SEMI-FINAL
26 October 1991, Murrayfield
Scotland 6
Penalty Goals G Hastings (2)

England 9
Penalty Goals Webb (2)
Dropped Goal Andrew

Scotland:
AG Hastings	DMB Sole (c)
	J Allan
AG Stanger	AP Burnell
S Hastings	
SRP Lineen	CA Gray
I Tukalo	GW Weir
	J Jeffrey
CM Chalmers	DB White
G Armstrong	F Calder

Referee: KVJ Fitzgerald (Australia)

England:
JM Webb	J Leonard
	BC Moore
SJ Halliday	JA Probyn
WDC Carling (c)	
JC Guscott	PJ Ackford
R Underwood	WA Dooley
	MG Skinner
CR Andrew	MC Teague
RJ Hill	PJ Winterbottom

WORLD CUP FINAL
2 November 1991, Twickenham
England 6

Penalty Goals Webb (2)

Australia 12
Try Daly
Conversion Lynagh
Penalty Goals Lynagh (2)

England:
JM Webb	J Leonard
	BC Moore
SJ Halliday	JA Probyn
WDC Carling (c)	
JC Guscott	PJ Ackford
R Underwood	WA Dooley
	MG Skinner
CR Andrew	MC Teague
RJ Hill	PJ Winterbottom

Referee: WD Bevan (Wales)

Australia:
MC Roebuck	AJ Daly
	PN Kearns
DI Campese	EJA McKenzie
JS Little	
TJ Horan	RJ McCall
RH Egerton	JA Eales
	SP Poidevin
MP Lynagh	V Ofahengaue
NC Farr-Jones (c)	T Coker

---

18 January 1992, Murrayfield
Scotland 7
Try White

Penalty Goal G Hastings

England 25
Tries Underwood, Morris
Conversion Webb
Penalty Goals Webb (4)
Dropped Goal Guscott

Scotland:
AG Hastings	DMB Sole (c)
	KS Milne
AG Stanger	AP Burnell
S Hastings	
SRP Lineen	NGB Edwards
I Tukalo	GW Weir
	IR Smith
CM Chalmers	DB White
AD Nicol	DJ McIvor

Referee: WD Bevan (Wales)

England:
JM Webb	J Leonard
	BC Moore
SJ Halliday	JA Probyn
WDC Carling (c)	
JC Guscott	MC Bayfield
R Underwood	WA Dooley
	MG Skinner
CR Andrew	TAK Rodber
CD Morris	PJ Winterbottom

Replacement:
D Richards (for Rodber)

1 February 1992, Twickenham

England 38
Tries Webb (2), Morris, Guscott, Underwood, Halliday
Conversions Webb (4)
Penalty Goals Webb (2)

Ireland 9
Try Keyes
Conversion Keyes
Penalty Goal Keyes

England:

JM Webb	J Leonard	JE Staples	NJ Popplewell
	BC Moore		SJ Smith
SJ Halliday	JA Probyn	RM Wallace	GF Halpin
WDC Carling (c)		BJ Mullin	
JC Guscott	MC Bayfield	DM Curtis	MJ Galwey
R Underwood	WA Dooley	SP Geoghegan	NPJ Francis
	MG Skinner		PM Matthews (c)
CR Andrew	TAK Rodber	RP Keyes	BF Robinson
CD Morris	PJ Winterbottom	F Aherne	MJ Fitzgibbon

Ireland:

Referee: WD Bevan (Wales)

---

15 February 1992, Parc des Princes, Paris

France 13
Tries Viars, Penaud
Conversion Viars
Penalty Goal Viars

England 31
Tries Webb, Underwood, Morris, penalty try
Conversions Webb (3)
Penalty Goals Webb (3)

France:

J-B Lafond	G Lascubé
	V Moscato
P Saint-André	P Gimbert
P Sella (c)	
F Mesnel	C Mougeot
S Viars	M Cecillon
	J-F Tordo
A Penaud	A van Heerden
F Galthié	L Cabannes

Replacements:
J-L Sadourny (for Sella)
O Roumat (for Mougeot)
P Montlaur (for Lafond)

England:

JM Webb	J Leonard
	BC Moore
SJ Halliday	JA Probyn
WDC Carling (c)	
JC Guscott	MC Bayfield
R Underwood	WA Dooley
	MG Skinner
CR Andrew	D Richards
CD Morris	PJ Winterbottom

Replacement:
D Pears (for Andrew)

Referee: SR Hilditch (Ireland)

---

7 March 1992, Twickenham

England 24
Tries Carling, Dooley, Skinner,
Conversions Webb (3)
Penalty Goals Webb (2)

Wales 0

England:

JM Webb	J Leonard
	BC Moore
SJ Halliday	JA Probyn
WDC Carling (c)	
JC Guscott	MC Bayfield
R Underwood	WA Dooley
	MG Skinner
CR Andrew	D Richards
CD Morris	PJ Winterbottom

Replacement:
NJ Heslop (for Carling)

Wales:

A Clement	M Griffiths
	GR Jenkins
IC Evans (c)	L Delaney
IS Gibbs	
NR Jenkins	AH Copsey
MR Hall	Gareth Llewellyn
	MS Morris
CJ Stephens	S Davies
RN Jones	RW Webster

Replacement:
M Rayer (for Clement)

Referee: RJ Megson (Scotland)

1992-93

17 October 1992, Wembley Stadium

England 26
Tries Hunter (2), Winterbottom, Guscott
Penalty Goals Webb (2)

Canada 13
Try Graf
Conversion Rees
Penalty Goals Rees (2)

England:

JM Webb	J Leonard	DS Stewart	EA Evans
	CJ Olver		KF Svoboda
I Hunter	VE Ubogu	SD Gray	DC Jackart
WDC Carling (c)		M Williams	
JC Guscott	WA Dooley	IC Stuart	J Knauer
T Underwood	MC Bayfield	DC Lougheed	N Hadley (c)
	D Ryan		I Gordon
CR Andrew	D Richards	GL Rees	C McKenzie
CD Morris	PJ Winterbottom	JD Graf	GI MacKinnon

Canada:

Replacement:
K Wirachowski (for Evans)

Referee: G Simmonds (Wales)

---

14 November 1992, Twickenham

England 33
Tries Carling, Guscott, Morris, T Underwood
Conversions Webb (2)
Penalty Goals Webb (3)

South Africa 16
Try Strauss
Conversion Botha
Penalty Goals Botha (2)
Dropped Goal Botha

England:

JM Webb	J Leonard	JTJ van Rensburg	JJ Styger
	BC Moore		WG Hills
T Underwood	VE Ubogu	JT Small	KS Andrews
WDC Carling (c)		DM Gerber	
JC Guscott	MC Bayfield	PG Müller	H Hattingh
R Underwood	WA Dooley	J Olivier	AW Malan
	MC Teague		CPStrauss
CR Andrew	BB Clarke	HE Botha (c)	A Richter
CD Morris	PJ Winterbottom	GD Wright	FC Smit

South Africa:

Replacement:
PR de Glanville (for T Underwood)

Referee: SR Hilditch (Ireland)

---

16 January 1993, Twickenham

England 16
Try Hunter
Conversion Webb
Penalty Goals Webb (3)

France 15
Tries Saint-André (2)
Conversion Camberabero
Penalty Goal Camberabero

England:

JM Webb	J Leonard	J-B Lafond	L Armary
	BC Moore		J-F Tordo (c)
I Hunter	JA Probyn	P Saint-André	L Seigne
WDC Carling (c)		P Sella	
JC Guscott	MC Bayfield	T Lacroix	A Benazzi
R Underwood	MO Johnson	P Hontas	O Roumat
	MC Teague		P Benetton
CR Andrew	BB Clarke	D Camberabero	M Cecillon
CD Morris	PJ Winterbottom	A Hueber	L Cabannes

France:

Replacements:
F Mesnel (for Sella)
S Ougier (for Lacroix)

Referee: JM Fleming (Scotland)

7 February 1993, Cardiff Arms Park
Wales 10   **England 9**
Try Evans
Conversion Jenkins
Penalty Goal Jenkins   *Penalty Goals* Webb (2)
                            Dropped Goal Guscott

Wales: **England:**
MA Rayer | RL Evans | JM Webb | J Leonard
 | N Meek | | BC Moore
IC Evans (c) | H Williams-Jones | I Hunter | JA Probyn
MR Hall | | WDC Carling (c) |
IS Gibbs | GO Llewellyn | JC Guscott | MC Bayfield
WT Proctor | AH Copsey | R Underwood | MO Johnson
 | EW Lewis | | MC Teague
NR Jenkins | S Davies | CR Andrew | BB Clarke
RN Jones | RE Webster | CD Morris | PJ Winterbottom
Replacement: PR de Glanville (for Hunter)
Referee: J Dumé (France)

6 March 1993, Twickenham
England 26   **Scotland 12**
Tries Guscott, R Underwood
T Underwood
Conversion Webb
Penalty Goals Webb (3)   *Penalty Goals* AG Hastings (3)
                            Dropped Goal Chalmers

England: | | **Scotland:**
JM Webb | J Leonard | AG Hastings (c) | PH Wright
 | BC Moore | | KS Milne
T Underwood | JA Probyn | AG Stanger | AP Burnell
WDC Carling (c) | | S Hastings |
JC Guscott | MC Bayfield | AG Shiel | AI Reed
R Underwood | WA Dooley | DA Stark | DF Cronin
 | MC Teague | | DJ Turnbull
S Barnes | BB Clarke | CM Chalmers | GW Weir
CD Morris | PJ Winterbottom | G Armstrong | IR Morrison
Replacement: GPJ Townsend (for Chalmers)
Referee: BW Stirling (Ireland)

20 March 1993, Lansdowne Road
Ireland 17   **England 3**
Try Galwey
Penalty Goals Elwood (2)   *Penalty Goal* Webb
Dropped Goals Elwood (2)

Ireland: | | **England:**
CP Clarke | NJ Popplewell | JM Webb | J Leonard
 | TJ Kingston | | BC Moore
RM Wallace | PM Clohessy | T Underwood | JA Probyn
VJG Cunningham | | WDC Carling (c) |
PPA Danaher | PS Johns | JC Guscott | MC Bayfield
SP Geoghegan | MJ Galwey | R Underwood | WA Dooley
 | PTJ O'Hara | | MC Teague
EP Elwood | BF Robinson | S Barnes | BB Clarke
MT Bradley (c) | WD McBride | CD Morris | PJ Winterbottom
Referee: AR MacNeill (Australia)

1993-94

27 November 1993, Twickenham
England 15   **New Zealand 9**
Penalty Goals Callard (4)   *Penalty Goals* Wilson (3)
Dropped Goal Andrew

England: | | **New Zealand:**
JEB Callard | J Leonard | JKR Timu | CW Dowd
 | BC Moore | | SBT Fitzpatrick (c)
T Underwood | VE Ubogu | JW Wilson | OM Brown
WDC Carling (c) | | FE Bunce |
PR de Glanville | MO Johnson | E Clarke | ID Jones
R Underwood | NC Redman | VL Tuigamala | SB Gordon
 | TAK Rodber | | JW Joseph
CR Andrew | D Richards | MCG Ellis | ARB Pene
KPP Bracken | BB Clarke | S Forster | ZV Brooke
Referee: F Burger (South Africa)

5 February 1994, Murrayfield
Scotland 14   **England 15**
Try Wainwright
Penalty Goals G Hastings (2)   *Penalty Goals* Callard (5)
Dropped Goal Townsend

Scotland: | | **England:**
AG Hastings (c) | AV Sharp | JEB Callard | J Leonard
 | KS Milne | | BC Moore
AG Stanger | AP Burnell | T Underwood | VE Ubogu
S Hastings | | WDC Carling (c) |
DS Wyllie | DS Munro | PR de Glanville | MC Bayfield
KM Logan | AI Reed | R Underwood | MO Johnson
 | P Walton | | JP Hall
GPJ Townsend | GW Weir | CR Andrew | BB Clarke
G Armstrong | RI Wainwright | KPP Bracken | NA Back
Replacements:
IC Jardine (for S Hastings)
BW Redpath (for Armstrong)
IR Smith (for Wainwright)
Referee: LL McLachlan (New Zealand)

19 February 1994, Twickenham
England 12   **Ireland 13**
                            Try Geoghegan
                            Conversion Elwood
Penalty Goals Callard (4)   *Penalty Goals* Elwood (2)

England: | | **Ireland:**
JEB Callard | J Leonard | CP O'Shea | NJ Popplewell
 | BC Moore | | TJ Kingston
T Underwood | VE Ubogu | RM Wallace | PM Clohessy
WDC Carling (c) | | MJ Field |
PR de Glanville | MO Johnson | PPA Danaher | MJ Galwey
R Underwood | MC Bayfield | SP Geoghegan | NPJ Francis
 | TAK Rodber | | BF Robinson
CR Andrew | SO Ojomoh | EP Elwood | PS Johns
KPP Bracken | NA Back | MT Bradley (c) | WD McBride
                          Replacement:
                          KD O'Connell (for Robinson)

Referee: P Thomas (France)

The Carling Years

5 March 1994, Parc des Princes
France 14   **England 18**
Try Benazzi
Penalty Goals Lacroix (3)   *Penalty Goals* Andrew (5)
                                                        Dropped Goal Andrew

France:
J-L Sadourny   L Bénézech
                             J-M Gonzales
W Téchoueyres   P Gallart
P Sella
T Lacroix   O Merle
P Saint-André   O Roumat (c)
                             A Benazzi
A Penaud   P Benetton
F Galthié   L Cabannes
Referee: SR Hilditch (Ireland)

England:
D Pears   J Leonard
                             BC Moore
I Hunter   VE Ubogu
WDC Carling (c)
PR de Glanville   MO Johnson
R Underwood   NC Redman
                             TAK Rodber
CR Andrew   SO Ojomoh
CD Morris   BB Clarke

19 March 1994, Twickenham
England 15   **Wales 8**
Tries R Underwood, Rodber   *Try* Walker
Conversion Andrew
Penalty Goal Andrew   *Penalty Goal* Jenkins

England:
I Hunter   J Leonard
                             BC Moore
T Underwood   VE Ubogu
WDC Carling (c)
PR de Glanville   MO Johnson
R Underwood   NC Redman
                             TAK Rodber
CR Andrew   D Richards
CD Morris   BB Clarke
Replacement:
MJ Catt (for Andrew)
Referee: JM Fleming (Scotland)

Wales:
MA Rayer   RL Evans
                             GR Jenkins
IC Evans (c)   JD Davies
MR Hall
NG Davies   GO Llewellyn
N Walker   PT Davies
                             EW Lewis
NR Jenkins   LS Quinnell
RHStJB Moon   MA Perego
Replacement:
AH Copsey (for Lewis)

4 June 1994, Loftus Versfeld, Pretoria
South Africa 15   **England 32**
                                                        Tries Clarke, Andrew
                                                        Conversions Andrew (2)
Penalty Goals Joubert (5)   *Penalty Goals* Andrew (5)
                                                        Dropped Goal Andrew

South Africa
AJ Joubert   A-H le Roux
                             J Allan
JT Small   IS Swart
PG Müller
B Venter   JJ Strydom
CM Williams   S Atherton
                             JF Pienaar (c)
HP le Roux   CP Strauss
JH van der Westhuizen FJ van Heerden

Referee: CJ Hawke (New Zealand)

England:
PA Hull   J Leonard
                             BC Moore
T Underwood   VE Ubogu
WDC Carling (c)
PR de Glanville   MC Bayfield
R Underwood   NC Redman
                             TAK Rodber
CR Andrew   D Richards
CD Morris   BB Clarke
Replacement:
SO Ojomoh (for Richards)

11 June 1994, Newlands, Cape Town
South Africa 27   **England 9**
Tries H le Roux, Joubert
Conversion Joubert
Penalty Goals H le Roux (3),   *Penalty Goals* Andrew (3)
Joubert (2)

South Africa:
AJ Joubert   JHS le Roux
                             J Allan
JT Small   IS Swart
PG Müller
B Venter   MG Andrews
CM Williams   S Atherton
                             JF Pienaar (c)
HP le Roux   A Richter
J Roux   I Macdonald
Replacements:
JH van der Westhuizen (for Williams)
FJ van Heerden (for Macdonald)
Referee: CJ Hawke (New Zealand)

England:
PA Hull   J Leonard
                             BC Moore
T Underwood   VE Ubogu
WDC Carling (c)
PR de Glanville   MC Bayfield
R Underwood   NC Redman
                             TAK Rodber
CR Andrew   BB Clarke
CD Morris   SO Ojomoh

1994-95

12 November 1994, Twickenham

England 54
Tries T Underwood (2), Carling, penalty try, Rodber, R Underwood
Conversions Andrew (6)
Penalty Goals Andrew (4)

Romania 3

Penalty Goal Ivanciuc

England:
PA Hull	J Leonard
	BC Moore
T Underwood	VE Ubogu
WDC Carling (c)	
JC Guscott	MO Johnson
R Underwood	MC Bayfield
	TAK Rodber
CR Andrew	BB Clarke
CD Morris	SO Ojomoh

Romania:
V Brici	L Costea
	I Negreci
G Solomie	G Vlad
M Vioreanu	C Cojocariu
IS Tofan	
R Cioca	C Branescu
	T Oroian
I Ivanciuc	T Brinza (c)
D Neaga	A Gealapu

Replacements:
C Draguceanu (for Oroian)
F Marioara (for Costea)
C Gheorghe (for Negreci)
A Guranescu (for Branescu)

Referee: S Neethling (South Africa)

10 December 1994, Twickenham

England 60
Tries T Underwood,
R Underwood (2), Bracken, Catt (2)
Conversions Andrew (6)
Penalty Goals Andrew (6)

Canada 19
Tries Lougheed (2), Evans

Conversions Rees (2)

England:
PA Hull	J Leonard
	BC Moore
T Underwood	VE Ubogu
WDC Carling (c)	
JC Guscott	MO Johnson
R Underwood	MC Bayfield
	TAK Rodber
CR Andrew	D Richards
KPP Bracken	BB Clarke

Canada:
DS Stewart	EA Evans
	ME Cardinal
R Toews	DC Jackart
C Stewart	
IC Stuart (c)	M James
DC Lougheed	N Hadley
	I Gordon
GL Rees	C McKenzie
JD Graf	GI MacKinnon

Replacements:
MJ Catt (for Hull)
PR de Glanville (for T Underwood)

Replacement:
SD Gray (for Stuart)

Referee: WJ Erickson (Australia)

21 January 1995, Lansdowne Road

Ireland 8
Try Foley

Penalty Goal Burke

England 20
Tries Carling, Clarke, T Underwood
Conversion Andrew
Penalty Goal Andrew

Ireland:
CMP O'Shea	NJ Popplewell
	KGM Wood
SP Geoghegan	PM Clohessy
BJ Mullin	
PPA Danaher	MJ Galwey
NKP Woods	NPJ Francis
	AG Foley
PA Burke	PS Johns
NA Hogan	D Corkery

England:
MJ Catt	J Leonard
	BC Moore
T Underwood	VE Ubogu
WDC Carling (c)	
JC Guscott	MO Johnson
R Underwood	MC Bayfield
	TAK Rodber
CR Andrew	D Richards
KPP Bracken	BB Clarke

Replacement:
GM Fulcher (for Francis)

Referee: P Thomas (France)

4 February 1995, Twickenham

England 31
Tries T Underwood (2), Guscott
Conversions Andrew (2)
Penalty Goals Andrew (4)

France 10
Try Viars
Conversion Lacroix
Penalty Goal Lacroix

England:
MJ Catt	J Leonard
	BC Moore
T Underwood	VE Ubogu
WDC Carling (c)	
JC Guscott	MO Johnson
R Underwood	MC Bayfield
	TAK Rodber
CR Andrew	D Richards
KPP Bracken	BB Clarke

France:
J-L Sadourny	L Bénézech
	J-M Gonzalez
P Bernat-Salles	C Califano
P Sella	
T Lacroix	O Brouzet
P Saint-André (c)	O Roumat
	A Benazzi
C Deylaud	P Benetton
G Accoceberry	L Cabannes

Replacements:
S Viars (for Sadourny)
M de Rougemont (for Gonzalez)*

Referee: KW McCartney (Scotland)

18 February 1995, Cardiff Arms Park

Wales 9

Penalty Goals Jenkins (3)

England 23
Tries R Underwood (2), Ubogu
Conversion Andrew
Penalty Goals Andrew (2)

Wales:
A Clement	M Griffiths
	GR Jenkins
IC Evans (c)	JD Davies
M Taylor	
NG Davies	GO Llewellyn
N Walker	D Jones
	HT Taylor
NR Jenkins	EW Lewis
RN Jones	RG Collins

Replacements:
RHStJB Moon (for Walker)
MJ Back (for Clement)
H Williams-Jones (for Taylor)

Referee: D Mene (France)

England:
MJ Catt	J Leonard
	BC Moore
T Underwood	VE Ubogu
WDC Carling (c)	
JC Guscott	MO Johnson
R Underwood	MC Bayfield
	TAK Rodber
CR Andrew	D Richards
KPP Bracken	BB Clarke

18 March 1995, Twickenham

England 24
Penalty Goals Andrew (7)
Dropped Goal Andrew

Scotland 12
Penalty Goals G Hastings (2)
Dropped Goals Chalmers (2)

England:
MJ Catt	J Leonard
	BC Moore
T Underwood	VE Ubogu
WDC Carling (c)	
JC Guscott	MO Johnson
R Underwood	MC Bayfield
	TAK Rodber
CR Andrew	D Richards
KPP Bracken	BB Clarke

Replacements:
SO Ojomoh (for Richards)
CD Morris (for Bracken)*
GC Rowntree (for Leonard)*

Scotland:
AG Hastings	DJW Hilton
	KS Milne
CA Joiner	PH Wright
GPJ Townsend	
S Hastings	GW Weir
KM Logan	SJ Campbell
	RI Wainwright
CM Chalmers	EW Peters
BW Redpath	IR Morrison

Replacement:
JJ Manson (for Hilton)

Referee: BW Stirling (Ireland)

WORLD CUP 1995

POOL B
27 May 1995, Durban
England 24

Argentina 18
Tries Noriega, Arbizu
Conversion Arbizu
Penalty Goals Arbizu (2)

Penalty Goals Andrew (6)
Dropped Goals Andrew (2)

England:
MJ Catt
J Leonard
BC Moore
T Underwood
VE Ubogu
WDC Carling (c)
JC Guscott
MO Johnson
R Underwood
MC Bayfield
TAK Rodber
CR Andrew
SO Ojomoh
CD Morris
BB Clarke
Replacement:
NA Back (for Ojomoh)*
Referee: JM Fleming (Scotland)

Argentina:
E Juardo
ME Corral
FE Mendez
MJ Teran
EP Noriega
D Cuesta Silva
S Salvat (c)
GA Llanes
D Albanese
PL Sporleder
R Martin
L Arbizu
JM Santamarina
RH Crexell
C Viel
Replacement:
S Irazoqui (for Viel)

---

31 May 1995, Durban
England 27
Tries R Underwood, T Underwood
Conversion Andrew
Penalty Goals Andrew (5)

Italy 20
Tries Vaccari, Massimo Cuttitta
Conversions Dominguez (2)
Penalty Goals Dominguez (2)

England:
MJ Catt
GC Rowntree
BC Moore
T Underwood
J Leonard
PR de Glanville
JC Guscott
MO Johnson
R Underwood
MC Bayfield
TAK Rodber
CR Andrew (c)
BB Clarke
KPP Bracken
NA Back
Referee: SR Hilditch (Ireland)

Italy:
L Troiani
Massimo Cuttita (c)
C Orlandi
P Vaccari
F Properzi-Curti
I Francescato
S Bordon
P Pedroni
M Gerosa
M Giacheri
O Arancio
D Dominguez
JM Gardner
A Troncon
A Sgorlon

---

4 June 1995, Durban
England 44
Tries Back, R Underwood (2), penalty try
Conversions Callard (3)
Penalty Goals Callard (5)
Dropped Goal Catt

Western Samoa 22
Tries Sini (2), Umaga

Conversions Fa'amasino (2)
Penalty Goal Fa'amasino

England:
JEB Callard
GC Rowntree
RGR Dawe
I Hunter
VE Ubogu
WDC Carling (c)
PR de Glanville
MO Johnson
R Underwood
R West
SO Ojomoh
MJ Catt
D Richards
CD Morris
NA Back
Replacements:
JA Mallett (for Rowntree)
TAK Rodber (for Back)
DP Hopley (for Carling)
BC Moore (for Richards)
KPP Bracken (for Rodber)
Referee: P Robin (France)

Western Samoa:
MT Umaga
MA Mika
T Leiasamaivo
B Lima
G Latu
T Vaega
T Fa'amasino
DR Williams
GE Leaupepe
L Falaniko
PL Leavasa
E Puleitu
PR Lam (c)
T Nu'uali'itia
M Iupeli
Replacements:
SJ Tatupu (for Leavasa)
F Sini (for Puleitu)
S Lemamea (for Tatupu)
P Fatialofa (for Latu)

QUARTER-FINAL
11 June 1995, Cape Town
England 25
Try T Underwood
Conversion Andrew
Penalty Goals Andrew (5)
Dropped Goal Andrew

Australia 22
Try Smith
Conversion Lynagh
Penalty Goals Lynagh (5)

England:
MJ Catt
J Leonard
BC Moore
T Underwood
VE Ubogu
WDC Carling (c)
JS Little
JC Guscott
MO Johnson
R Underwood
MC Bayfield
TAK Rodber
CR Andrew
D Richards
CD Morris
BB Clarke
Replacement:
SO Ojomoh (for Richards)*
Referee: DJ Bishop (New Zealand)

Australia:
M Burke
DJ Crowley
PN Kearns (c)
DI Campese
EJA McKenzie
TJ Horan
RJ McCall
DP Smith
JA Eales
V Ofahengaue
MP Lynagh
BT Gavin
GM Gregan
DJ Wilson

SEMI-FINAL
18 June 1995, Cape Town
New Zealand 45
Tries Lomu (4), Kronfeld, Bachop
Conversions Mehrtens (3)
Penalty Goal Mehrtens
Dropped Goals Z Brooke, Mehrtens

England 29
Tries R Underwood (2), Carling (2)
Conversions Andrew (3)
Penalty Goal Andrew

New Zealand:
GM Osborne
CW Dowd
SBT Fitzpatrick (c)
JW Wilson
OM Brown
FE Bunce
WK Little
ID Jones
JT Lomu
RM Brooke
MR Brewer
AP Mehrtens
ZV Brooke
GTM Bachop
JA Kronfeld
Replacement:
BP Larsen (for Z Brooke)
Referee: SR Hilditch (Ireland)

England:
MJ Catt
J Leonard
BC Moore
T Underwood
VE Ubogu
WDC Carling (c)
JC Guscott
MO Johnson
R Underwood
MC Bayfield
TAK Rodber
CR Andrew
D Richards
CD Morris
BB Clarke

THIRD PLACE PLAY-OFF
22 June 1995, Pretoria
France 19
Tries Roumat, Ntamack
Penalty Goals Lacroix (3)

England 9

Penalty Goals Andrew (3)

France:
J-L Sadourny
L Bénézech
J-M Gonzalez
E Ntamack
C Califano
P Sella
T Lacroix
O Merle
P Saint-André (c)
O Roumat
A Benazzi
F Mesnel
A Cigagna
F Galthié
L Cabannes
Referee: DJ Bishop (New Zealand)

England:
MJ Catt
J Leonard
BC Moore
I Hunter
VE Ubogu
WDC Carling (c)
JC Guscott
MO Johnson
R Underwood
MC Bayfield
TAK Rodber
CR Andrew
SO Ojomoh
CD Morris
BB Clarke

1995-96

18 November 1995, Twickenham

England 14
Try de Glanville
Penalty Goals Callard (3)

South Africa 24
Tries Williams (2), van der Westhuizen
Penalty Goals Stransky (3)

England:
JEB Callard	J Leonard
	MP Regan
DP Hopley	VE Ubogu
WDC Carling (c)	
JC Guscott	MO Johnson
R Underwood	MC Bayfield
	TAK Rodber
MJ Catt	BB Clarke
KPP Bracken	RA Robinson

Replacements:
LBN Dallaglio (for Rodber)
PR de Glanville (for Carling)
Referee: J Fleming (Scotland)

South Africa:
AJ Joubert	A van der Linde
	J Dalton
J Olivier	TG Laubscher
JC Mulder	
HP Le Roux	KJJ Wiese
CM Williams	MG Andrews
	RJ Kruger
JT Stransky	FJ van Heerden
JH van der Westhuizen	JF Pienaar (c)

Replacements:
JT Small (for Olivier)
RAW Straeuli (for Kruger)

16 December 1995, Twickenham

England 27
Tries Dallaglio, Underwood
Conversion Grayson
Penalty Goals Grayson (5)

Western Samoa 9

Penalty Goals Kellett (3)

England:
MJ Catt	GC Rowntree
	MP Regan
DP Hopley	J Leonard
WDC Carling (c)	
JC Guscott	MO Johnson
R Underwood	MC Bayfield
	TAK Rodber
PJ Grayson	BB Clarke
MJS Dawson	LBN Dallaglio

Referee: I Rogers (South Africa)

Western Samoa:
V Patu	MA Mika
	T Leiasamaiva'o
B Lima	P Fatialofa
T Vaega	
G Leaupepe	P Leavasa
A Telea	F Falaniko
	S Kaleta
D Kellett	P Lam (c)
J Filemu	S Vaifale

Replacement:
S Smith (for Filemu)

20 January 1996, Parc des Princes, Paris

France 15
Penalty Goals Lacroix (3)
Dropped Goals Lacroix, Castaignède

England 12
Penalty Goals Grayson (2)
Dropped Goals Grayson (2)

France :
J-L Sadourny	M Périé
	J-M Gonzalez
E Ntamack	C Califano
R Dourthe	
T Castaignède	O Roumat
P Saint-André (c)	O Merle
	A Benazzi
T Lacroix	F Pelous
P Carbonneau	L Cabannes

Replacement:
P Bernat-Salles (for Sadourny)
Referee: D McHugh (Ireland)

England:
MJ Catt	GC Rowntree
	MP Regan
JM Sleightholme	J Leonard
WDC Carling (c)	
JC Guscott	MO Johnson
R Underwood	MC Bayfield
	SO Ojomoh
PJ Grayson	BB Clarke
MJS Dawson	LBN Dallaglio

Replacement:
D Richards (for Clarke)*

3 February 1996, Twickenham

England 21
Tries Underwood, Guscott
Conversion Grayson
Penalty Goals Grayson (3)

Wales 15
Tries Taylor, Howley
Conversion Thomas
Penalty Goal Thomas

England:
MJ Catt	GC Rowntree
	MP Regan
JM Sleightholme	J Leonard
WDC Carling (c)	
JC Guscott	MO Johnson
R Underwood	MC Bayfield
	TAK Rodber
PJ Grayson	BB Clarke
MJS Dawson	LBN Dallaglio

Replacement:
PR de Glanville (for Carling)
Referee: KW McCartney (Scotland)

Wales:
WJL Thomas	ALP Lewis
	JM Humphreys (c)
IC Evans	JD Davies
L Davies	
NG Davies	GO Llewellyn
WT Proctor	D Jones
	EW Lewis
AC Thomas	HT Taylor
R Howley	RG Jones

Replacement:
GR Jenkins (for Humphreys)

16 March 1996, Murrayfield

Scotland 9
Penalty Goals Dods (3)

England 18
Penalty Goals Grayson (6)

Scotland:
RJS Shepherd	DJW Hilton
	KD McKenzie
CA Joiner	PH Wright
S Hastings	
IC Jardine	GW Weir
M Dods	SJ Campbell
	RI Wainwright (c)
GPJ Townsend	EW Peters
BW Redpath	IR Smith

Referee: WD Bevan (Wales)

England:
MJ Catt	GC Rowntree
	MP Regan
JM Sleightholme	J Leonard
WDC Carling (c)	
JC Guscott	MO Johnson
R Underwood	GS Archer
	BB Clarke
PJ Grayson	D Richards
MJS Dawson	LBN Dallaglio

Replacement:
TAK Rodber (for Richards)

16 March 1996, Twickenham

England 28
Try Sleightholme
Conversion Grayson
Penalty Goals Grayson (6)
Dropped Goal Grayson

Ireland 15

Penalty Goals Mason (4)
Dropped Goal Humphreys

England:
MJ Catt	GC Rowntree
	MP Regan
JM Sleightholme	J Leonard
WDC Carling (c)	
JC Guscott	MO Johnson
R Underwood	GS Archer
	BB Clarke
PJ Grayson	D Richards
MJS Dawson	LBN Dallaglio

Replacement:
PR de Glanville (for Carling)
Referee: E Murray (Scotland)

Ireland:
SJP Mason	NJ Popplewell
	ATH Clarke
SP Geoghegan	PS Wallace
JC Bell	
MJ Field	GM Fulcher
NKJP Woods	JW Davidson
	DS Corkery
DG Humphreys	VCP Costello
NA Hogan (c)	WD McBride

Replacement:
CM McCall (for Field)

* denotes appearance as temporary replacement

Roll of Honour: 1988–96

ACKFORD PJ
1988: A; 1989: S, I, F, W, R, Fij; 1990: I, F, W, S, Bar†, Arg; 1991: W, S, I, F, A, [NZ, It, F, S, A].

ANDREW CR
1988: A; 1989: S, I, F, W, R, Fij; 1990: I, F, W, S, It†, Bar†, Arg; 1991: W, S, I, F, Fij, A, [NZ, It, USA, F, S, A]; 1992: S, I, F, W, C, SA; 1993: F, W, NZ; 1994: S, I, F, W, SA, SA, R, C; 1995: I, F, W, S,[Arg, It, A, NZ, F]

ARCHER GS
1996: S, I

BACK NA
1990: It†; 1994: S, I; 1995: [Arg, It, WS]

BAILEY MD
1989: Fij; 1990: I, F, S

BARNES S
1993: S, I

BATES SM
1989: R; 1990: It†

BAYFIELD MC
1991: Fij, A; 1992: S, I, F, W, C, SA; 1993: F, W, S, I; 1994 S, I, SA, SA, R, C; 1995: I, F, W, S, [Arg, It, A, NZ, F], SA, WS; 1996: F, W

BRACKEN KPP
1993: NZ; 1994: S, I, C; 1995: I, F, W, S, [Arg, WS,] SA

BUCKTON JDR
1988: A; 1990: It†, Arg

CALLARD JEB
1993: NZ; 1994: S, I; 1995: [WS]; 1996: SA

CARLING WDC
1988: A; 1989: S, I, F, W, Fij; 1990: It†, Arg, Arg, Bar†, Arg; 1991: W, S, I, F, Fij, A, [NZ, It, USA, F, S, A]; 1992: S, I, F, W, C, SA; 1993: F, W, S, I, NZ; 1994: S, I, F, W, SA, SA, R, C; 1995: I, F, W, S, [Arg, WS, A, NZ, F], SA, WS; 1996: F, W, S, I

CATT MJ
1994: W; 1995: I, F, W, S, [Arg, It, WS, A, NZ], SA, WS; 1996: F, W, S, I

CHILCOTT GJ
1989: I, W, R

CLARKE BB
1992: SA; 1993: F, W, S, I, NZ; 1994: S, F, W, SA, SA, R, C; 1995: I, F, W, S, [Arg, It, A, NZ, F], SA, WS; 1996: F, W, S, I

CLOUGH JF
1990: It*

CUSANI DA
1990: It†

DALLAGLIO LBN
1995: SA, WS; 1996: F, W, S, I

DAWE RGR
1995: [WS]

DAWSON MJS
1995: WS; 1996: F, W, S, I

de GLANVILLE PR
1992: SA; 1993: W, NZ; 1994: S, I, F, W, SA, SA, C; 1995: [It, WS], SA; 1996: W, I

DOOLEY WA
1988: A; 1989: S. I, F, W, R, Fij; 1990: I, F, W, S, It†, Arg, Arg, Bar†, Arg; 1991: W, S, I, F, [NZ, USA, F, S, A]; 1992: S, I, F, W, C, SA; 1993: S, I

EGERTON DW
1988: A; 1989: Fij; 1990: I, Arg

GRAYSON PJ
1995: WS; 1996: F, W, S, I

GUSCOTT JC
1989: R; 1990: I, F, W, S, Bar†, Arg; 1991: W, S, I, F, Fij, A, [NZ, It, F, S, A]; 1992: S, I, F, W, C, SA; 1993: F, W, S, I; 1994: R, C; 1995: I, F, W, S, [Arg, It, A, NZ, F], SA, WS; 1996: F, W, S, I

HALL JP
1990: Arg; 1994: S

HALLIDAY SJ
1988: A; 1989: S, I, F, W, R; 1990: W, S; 1991: [USA, S, A]; 1992: S, I, F, W

HARRIMAN AT
1988: A

HESLOP NJ
1990: It†, Arg, Arg, Arg; 1991: W, S, I, F, [USA, F]; 1992: W

HILL RJ
1989: Fij; 1990: I, F, W, S, Arg, Arg, Bar†, Arg; 1991: W, S, I, F, Fij, A, [NZ, It, USA, F, S, A]

HODGKINSON SD
1989: R, Fij; 1990: I, F, W, S, It†, Arg, Arg, Bar†, Arg; 1991: W, S, I, F, [USA]

HOPLEY DP
1995: [WS]; 1996: SA, WS

HULL PA
1994: SA, SA, R, C

HUNTER I
1992: C; 1993: F, W; 1994: F, W; 1995: [WS, F]

JOHNSON MO
1993: F, W, NZ; 1994: S, I, F, W, R, C; 1995: I, F, W, S, [Arg, It, WS, A, NZ, F], SA, WS; 1996: F, W, S, I

KIMMINS R
1990: It†

LEONARD J
1990: Arg, Arg, Bar†, Arg; 1991: W, S, I, F, Fij, A, [NZ, It, USA, F, S, A]; 1992: S, I, F, W, C, SA; 1993: F, W, S, I, NZ; 1994: S, I, F, W, SA, SA, R, C; 1995: I, F, W, S, [Arg, It, A, NZ, F], SA, WS; 1996: F, W, S, I

LINNETT MS
1989: Fij; 1990: It†

MALLETT JA
1995: [WS]

MOORE BC
1988: A; 1989: S, I, F, W, R, Fij; 1990: I, F, W, S, It†, Arg, Arg; 1991: W, S, I, F, Fij, A, [NZ, It, F, S, A]; 1992: S, I, F, W, SA; 1993: F, W, S, I, NZ; 1994: S, I, F, W, SA, SA, R, C; 1995: I, F, W, S, [Arg, It, WS, A, NZ, F]

MORRIS CD
1988: A; 1989: S, I, F, W; 1992: S, I, F, W, C; 1993: F, W, S, I; 1994: F, W, SA, SA, R; 1995: [Arg, WS, A, NZ, F]

MULLINS AR
1989: Fij

OJOMOH SO
1994: I, F, SA, SA, R; 1995: S, [Arg, WS, A, F]; 1996: F

OLVER CJ
1990: It†, Bar†, Arg; 1991: [USA]; 1992: C

OTI C
1989: S, I, F, W, R; 1990: It†, Arg, Arg; 1991: Fij, A, [NZ, It]

PEARCE GS
1991: [USA]

PEARS D
1990: Arg, Arg; 1992: F; 1994: F

PROBYN JA
1988: A; 1989: S, I, F, R; 1990: I, F, W, S, It†, Arg, Arg, Bar†, Arg; 1991: W, A, I, F, Fij, A, [NZ, It, F, S, A]; 1992: S, I, F, W; 1993: F, W, S, I

REDMAN NC
1990: Arg, Arg; 1991: Fij, [It, USA]; 1993: NZ; 1994: F, W, SA, SA

REES GW
1989: W, R; 1990: Bar†, Arg; 1991: Fij, [USA]

REGAN MP
1995: SA, WS; 1996: F, W, S, I

RENDALL PAG
1988: A; 1989: S, I, F, W, R; 1990: I, F, W, S; 1991: [It]

RICHARDS D
1988: A; 1989: S, I, F, W, R; 1990: Bar†, Arg; 1991: W, S, I, F, Fij, A, [NZ, It, USA]; 1992: S, W, F, C; 1993: NZ; 1994: W, SA, C; 1995: I, F, W, S, [WS, A, NZ]; 1996: S, I

ROBINSON RA
1988: A; 1989: S, I, F, W; 1995: SA

RODBER TAK
1992: S, I; 1993: NZ; 1994: I, F, W, SA, SA, R, C; 1995: I, F, W, S, [Arg, It, WS, A, NZ, F], SA, WS; 1996: W, S

ROWNTREE GC
1995: [It, WS], WS; 1996: F, W, S, I

RYAN D
1990: Arg, Arg; 1992: C

SKINNER MG
1989: Fij; 1990: I, F, W, S, Arg, Arg; 1991: Fij, [USA, F, S, A]; 1992: S, I, F, W

SLEIGHTHOLME JM
1996: F, W, S, I

TEAGUE MC
1989: S, I, F, W, R; 1990: F, W, S, Bar†; 1991: W, S, I, F, Fij, A, [NZ, It, F, S, A]; 1992: SA; 1993: F, W, S, I

UBOGU VE
1992: C, SA; 1993: NZ; 1994: S, I, F, W, SA, SA, R, C; 1995: I, F, W, S, [Arg, It, A, NZ, F], SA, WS

UNDERWOOD T
1990: Bar†; 1992: C, SA; 1993: S, I, NZ; 1994, S, I, W, SA, SA, R, C; 1995: I, F, W, S, [Arg, It, A, NZ]

UNDERWOOD R
1988: A; 1989: S, I, F, W, R, Fij; 1990: I, F, W, S, Bar†, Arg; 1991: W, S, I, F, Fij, A, [NZ, It, USA, F, S, A]; 1992: S, I, F, W, SA; 1993: F, W, S, I, NZ; 1994: S, I, F, W, SA, SA, R, C; 1995: I, F, W, S, [Arg, It, WS, A, NZ, F], SA, WS; 1996: F, W, S, I

WEBB JM
1988: A; 1989: S, I, F, W; 1991: Fij, A, [NZ, It, F, S, A]; 1992: S, I, F, W, C, SA; 1993: F, W, S, I

WELLS J
1990: It†

WEST R
1995: [WS]

WINTERBOTTOM PJ
1989: R, Fij; 1990: I, F, W, S, Arg, Arg, Bar†, Arg; 1991: W, S, I, F, A, [NZ, It, F, S, A]; 1992: S, I, F, W, C, SA; 1993: F, W, S, I

KEY: A: Australia, Arg: Argentina; Bar: Barbarians; C: Canada; F: France; Fij: Fiji; I: Ireland; It: Italy; NZ: New Zealand; R: Romania; S: Scotland; USA: United States of America; W: Wales; WS: Western Samoa; † denotes a non-cap international; [ ] denotes games played in the Rugby World Cup.

Top Ten Point Scorers: 1988–96	
296	CR Andrew
225	SD Hodgkinson
216	R Underwood
194	JM Webb
81	PJ Grayson
79	JC Guscott
69	JEB Callard
50	WDC Carling
	T Underwood
24	C Oti

Top Ten Try Scorers: 1988–96	
38	R Underwood
17	JC Guscott
12	WDC Carling
10	T Underwood
5	CD Morris
4	JM Webb
3	CR Andrew
	I Hunter
	JA Probyn
	D Richards
	MG Skinner
	NJ Heslop